#14 $\frac{95}{60.9}$

Vernon from
Grandma   Xmas 88

FRED WICHE'S
GARDENING
ALMANAC

CONTENTS

Fred Wiche's Gardening
Almanac

Compiled by Bob Hill

Design and production by
Stephen Sebree

Edited by Jena Monahan

Cover photograph
by Gary S. Chapman

Assistants to the project:
Jenny Wiche
Janet Hill
Debbie Sebree

Copyright © 1988 by Green
Thumb Publishing

Published by Green Thumb
Publishing
P.O. Box 3703
Louisville, Kentucky 40201

Printed by The Merrick Printing
Company Inc.

Library of Congress Catalog
Card Number: 88-82976

ISBN 0-9621352-0-8

This book is dedicated to the
best partner any man has ever
had—my wife Jenny.
  She has been a constant source
of inspiration. Without her help
and counsel the idea for the
Weekend Gardener would never
have germinated.

Welcome to "Fred Wiche's Gardening Almanac." It grew, so to speak, from the thousands of questions I've been asked over the years by people who were unsure about what to do when in their gardens.

To help answer those questions, this book has been specifically arranged as a month-to-month gardening guide. It will explain what you should be doing every month of the year; when to plant, prune or fertilize.

Each month has been divided into roughly three 10-day sections; early, middle and late. These sections, by necessity, are only **general guidelines**. No two gardening years are ever the same. One April will be colder than the next, or a hot, dry summer, such as in 1988, may throw your plants off schedule.

You'll also see some repetition in the book, but that's by design; there are many gardening tasks that must be done more than once a year.

My gardening experience, both on and off the air, has taught me that there is no one best way to do anything. My rule of thumb is that for every gardening rule there are 25 exceptions. Your best guide, as always, is common sense.

I've also learned that you can never tell a gardener that something can't be done. One year on the Milton Metz radio show I was asked about growing head lettuce here. I said it couldn't be done, to stick to leaf lettuce or semi-heading lettuce. A month later I stopped counting after the 14th basket of head lettuce arrived at the studio, each with an attached note saying, "Oh, yeah!"

I have mostly stayed away from recommending specific varieties of vegetables, flowers or shrubs because they are often upgraded or changed. I do mention specific pesticides and fungicides, but they are subject to change or even government recall, so stay tuned to all forms of gardening information.

I would like to thank many people, including my friends at the University of Kentucky, Purdue University, Ohio State University, the University of Illinois and those with the U.S. Department of Agriculture, who helped supply much of this information.

I hope you have as much fun reading the book as we had putting it together.

Fred Wiche
The Weekend Gardener.

JANUARY

JANUARY CHECKLIST

EARLY

☐ Turn Christmas tree into a bird feeder.
☐ Plant living Christmas trees.
☐ Continue watering evergreens.
☐ Decide whether to keep Christmas plants or discard them.
☐ Water and fertilize poinsettias and Christmas cactuses.
☐ Check trees for rodent damage.

MIDDLE

☐ Force early flowering trees and shrubs to bloom indoors.
☐ Draw detailed maps of what you would like to do to lawn and garden area.
☐ Check stored bulbs for rot.
☐ Increase humidity around houseplants.
☐ Bring spring-flowering bulbs out of cold storage for blooming indoors.

LATE

☐ Check plants for damage done by salt.
☐ Repot root-bound asparagus fern and other ferns.
☐ Have lawn mower tuned up and extra blades sharpened.

SUPER TIP

☐ Raising healthy houseplants.

January may be a slow month for gardening, but it's a great time to begin taking basketball seriously, and that will cover a lot of ground.

January is named for the Roman god Janus, a deity who was pictured with two heads and was thus able to see into the past and the future. It also made him the perfect guy to usher in the new year.

The average high temperature in January in Kentuckiana is 40.8 degrees. The average low is 24.1 degrees. The average precipitation is 3.38 inches, much of it white. That's because "melted snowfall" is also included in precipitation totals — with 10 inches of snow roughly equal to one inch of rain. The average snowfall for January, by the way, is 5.2 inches.

The most precipitation ever to fall on Louisville in January came in 1937, when an astounding 19.17 inches — all of it rain — dropped in. That has since been called, with some reverence, the '37 Flood.

The least precipitation ever to fall in the month was .45 inches, which occurred in 1981. The worst snowstorm in Louisville history dropped 15.7 inches on the city on Jan. 16 and 17 during the awful winter of 1978.

The warmest January day in history occurred in 1943, when the temperature rose to 79 degrees on Jan. 24. The coldest day in the Louisville area was, oddly enough, exactly 20 years later when the temperature on Jan. 24, 1963, dropped to 20 degrees below zero. The thermometer also hit minus 20 in 1884, but who can remember that?

The coldest day in Kentucky history was Jan. 28, 1963, when the temperature dropped to 34 degrees below zero in Cynthiana and Bonnieville.

There are nine hours and 34 minutes of sunlight on Jan. 1, which increases to 10 hours and 15 minutes by Jan. 31. Average soil temperatures — taken at a depth of four inches below a sod cover — range from 33 to 40 degrees.

The late, great Millard Fillmore, who for a president would have made a great gardener, was born Jan. 7, 1800.

EARLY

Yes, it's best to get your Christmas tree out of the house before Valentine's Day. Now is the time to do something useful with it; turn it into a bird feeder.

It will provide some bird cover in your back yard, and if you attach suet, molded seeds or the hanging bird-food "bells" you can find at most stores, you'll help the bird.

If you don't want to feed the birds, cutting off the limbs of the tree will provide you with good mulch for perennial flower beds, especially fall-planted mums.

If you were given a living Christmas tree, be sure to get it in the ground by early January and keep it well-watered. Its roots won't have a chance to grow in this weather and it could dry out and die very quickly. Don't keep it in the house for more than 10 days.

If possible, and this certainly depends on the weather, keep watering your evergreen plants, especially newly planted ones. If the ground is frozen, watch for the first available time to water.

This is the time to decide if you want to keep your Christmas plants or discard them. The Christmas pepper and Jerusalem cherry will not flower again and should be tossed out. But your poinsettia, holiday cactus and cyclamen should bloom until February or even longer.

Give the poinsettia a sunny, cool location and water when the soil is dry. About mid-March prune the stems from three to six inches to remove the colored bracts, and fertilize the plant. Move it outdoors in warm weather, and late next September begin to alternate sun and total darkness to induce blooming again. You'll read more about that in later chapters.

With cactus — and this works for the Thanksgiving cactus as well as the Christmas cactus — give the plant a sunny, cool home indoors, water two to four days AFTER the soil is dry and fertilize each month until May.

Place it outdoors in June, water and fertilize until August. About Sept. 1 cut the watering in half, but try to leave the cactus outdoors until about Oct. 15. It needs the cool nights to trigger the flowering, but keep it protected from frost. After Oct. 15, give it a sunny location indoors and enjoy the flowers.

You should be making periodic trips around the yard checking young trees for rodent damage on the lower trunks. It's still not too late to protect them with hardware cloth or protective collars. There's nothing worse than to walk around the yard on the first nice day of spring and notice that the rodents have eaten the bark off your baby trees.

MIDDLE

If you're hungering for fresh blooms, early flowering trees and shrubs such as forsythia, crab apple, flowering quince, flowering dogwood and honeysuckle can be forced to bloom indoors by cutting off the branches and placing them indoors in warm water.

Since the seed catalogs come earlier every year, you should have a stack as high as the Christmas bills by now. We talk a lot about planning, but it's so vital to a well-landscaped lawn and healthy garden.

Think about what went wrong last year, what went right, and what you'd like to add or change. Draw detailed maps. Shut your eyes and see the even flow of colors, the subtle mix of evergreens and azaleas, the dogwood and the flowering pear. Then plan accordingly. Dreaming, at least, is free.

Check those stored canna, gladiolus, dahlia and other tender bulbs you dug up last fall for signs of rot or excess moisture. Throw out the sick ones.

Try to increase the humidity around your houseplants, if not with watering pans then with a humidifier. A humidifier would be worth the investment if you plan to have healthy plants for a long time. It would keep you from drying up, too.

If you potted spring-flowering bulbs last October or November, you can bring a few out of cold storage now to begin the process of having them flower indoors. Place them in a cool, sunny area and add a little water.

LATE

This is the time of year when salt damage begins to show up on your plants as work crews salt the roads to make the drive home easier. The evidence is on the evergreen trees and bushes that show severe burn on one side, while the other side is deep forest green because the roots haven't been damaged.

Other indicators include stunting, dieback of the tips, leaf burn and leaf drop.

Some plants are more susceptible than others; cedars and white pines, for example, are more apt to be affected than Scotch and Austrian pines.

Among deciduous trees, oaks and sugar maples are more apt to be damaged, but the damage can't be seen until late in the spring when they leaf out.

Once the salt is in the trees, there isn't much you can do except try to keep the trees well-watered to leach out the salt. Be sure to fertilize them this spring.

Now is a good time to repot your root-bound asparagus fern, or the other ferns that seem to have stopped growing or are so thirsty they suck up every drop of water you give them in a few hours. You can grow the new divisions through the rest of the winter and surprise friends with a nice gift.

A pot-bound fern will have roots climbing all over the inside of the pot in a white mass. To help it, cut the rootball into halves, or even quarters, from top to bottom. Make clean cuts with a sharp knife to avoid too much root damage. Each slice should include a proportionate amount of foliage.

Gently untangle the matted roots so they will spread out in the new container. Place a few inches of sterile, well-drained potting soil in the new container and spread the root system over it. Fill in the rest, watering as you go to suck the soil down around the roots.

Remember those garden resolutions you made at the start of last season? Have you kept them? Have you taken your lawn mower or tiller to the shop for a tuneup? Don't forget to take extra blades for sharpening as well. A tuneup now will avoid weeks of waiting when it matters.

Are you saving your old motor oil to dump into a bucket of sand to clean your tools? And this year, buy a putty knife and keep it where you store the mower. Use it to clean the underside after every use. Disconnect the spark plug first.

FRED'S TIPS

Keep the leaves of your houseplants away from windows. One brush against frozen glass can injure, or even kill, your plants.

Here are some nifty tips I found in National Gardening magazine that will give you something to do this month, as well as help get rid of those ubiquitous plastic milk jugs. Save them and:

■ Cut strips from the flat center portion to be used as plant labels.

■ Cut off the bottom third of the jug for saucers or seed-starter trays.

■ Cut off just the bottom surface to create a mini-greenhouse to protect new transplants in the garden.

■ Remove the cap and cut off the bottom. Bury this "funnel" upside down next to a squash or pumpkin hill for fast, deep watering. Just fill the funnel and let the water trickle out.

You can also save those plastic, pint-sized berry baskets to protect newly sprouted seedlings in the spring, or use them to support melons and squash as they mature. It will keep them off the ground and away from bacteria.

You can also make your own seed tapes — those long strips of tape with seeds already attached at proper intervals — to kill some time on a January day. It's the perfect thing to do with a child whom you're trying to interest in gardening.

All you need is seeds, flour and water, single-ply toilet paper and toothpicks. Make a flour and water paste thick enough to stick to a toothpick.

Roll out the paper. Spread seeds out on another piece of paper, dip the toothpick into the paste and then touch a seed. It will stick to the toothpick. Now place the seed on the toilet paper. Repeat this procedure, leaving the distance recommended on the seed package between the seeds. Let it dry, mark and store. When planted underground this spring, the paper and paste will disintegrate.

Try using sand, cat litter, ashes or even fertilizer as a de-icing agent on your sidewalk. Just don't overdo it; even they can cause damage. Too much fertilizer can be as unhealthy as too little.

If you don't have a "cold frame" to help you get the garden started early, give some thought to building one. They need not be elaborate; a square of treated lumber covered with plastic or an old storm window will do. But they can get your season started weeks earlier. You can also buy automatic openers for the cold frame lids that will prevent your plants from being fried on a sudden warm, sunny day. Check the catalogs and nurseries. If an opener saves one crop, it's almost paid for itself.

Here's another tip to occupy a winter weekend; try planting a terrarium — or "plants in a bottle." A terrarium can be fun, and because the plants provide their own environment, a terrarium is easy to care for — provided you get started correctly.

There are whole books on the subject, and you should buy one. Be sure to look around for exotic bottles, including the big ones once used for water supplies in company offices. Check the flea markets and antique stores.

I receive phone calls from newer gardeners periodically wanting me to clarify the meaning of "hybrid" in the seed catalogs.

Hybrid in a seed catalog means the first generation seed from a cross produced by combining two parent plants. It's done through controlled pollination to produce a new variety that is uniform and stable in the first generation.

These are called FI hybrids and must be created anew each year from crosses between breeding-stock parents. If you allow hybrid plants to go to seed and then plant that seed, you will not get many plants like the immediate parents. You get throwbacks to previous generations, which

can be quite complex.

Therefore, every summer I get calls from gardeners wanting me to identify some strange-looking squash plant. I can't, because they planted seeds from hybrids grown the previous year. The offspring could look like anybody in the family.

Snow serves as an insulator and protects many plants from cold temperatures and drying winds. If it hangs on limbs, it must be removed very carefully — if at all — or you may break the limbs. Snow around the base of a bush, however, is a great help. Leave ice on tree limbs alone. It must melt naturally, or you'll damage the limbs.

I like to buy most of my seeds from local gardening centers, often after checking their colors and characteristics in the brightly colored catalogs we receive from seed companies.

If you do buy via the U.S. Mail, here are a few tips:

■ Buy from a reputable firm.

■ Don't be misled by fantastic claims; if it sounds too good to be true, it is. And fast-growing plants are often the weakest; a tree that goes up quickly often falls apart quickly. Read the descriptions carefully.

■ Temperatures in our area

sometimes fall to well below zero, so be sure to order plants hardy to this area.

■ Keep a copy of your order. Pay by check or credit card. Keep track of the guarantee policy and use it.

You'll get more birds if you place your feeder near trees, shrubs or other natural cover. To that point, many people, myself included, have often said that if you begin feeding the birds, you shouldn't stop or they may starve.

But I recently received a letter from Dr. John S. Castrale with the Indiana Department of Natural Resources, who said there is no basis for believing that.

"Wintering birds are very opportunistic," he wrote, "and are attracted to feeders because food is available. If your feeder runs out of food, birds will look elsewhere. . . ."

Castrale added that many people are afraid to begin feeding the birds because they think that if they stop or leave on vacation, the birds will die, which is not true.

What's important, he said, is to feed the birds during harsh weather, especially after a deep snow, and to buy quality seeds like those available from the lo-

cal Audubon Society. Millet of various kinds, he said, should be the most important ingredient in commercially grown seeds.

FRED'S SUPER TIP

There's no part of gardening that requires more plain ol' trial and error than raising houseplants. The novice often runs into a bewildering array of warnings about too much light, not enough light, too much water, not enough water, too much fertilizer, etc.

Houseplants do take care, especially to keep them healthy indoors in the winter. But they're well worth the trouble. Here is a general outline of what to do.

Buy a good, general information book on raising houseplants, especially one that gives the light, temperature and water requirements of each plant. Whatever it costs, it will save you a lot of money.

All plants need light, and that can be easily supplied with artificial lights if the sun can't reach around the corner by the stairs. Be sure the light is no less than six to eight inches away and have it on at least 16 hours a day. Just plain old cool-white fluorescent lights will work, and they're much cheaper than fancy plant lights.

Indoor houseplants can be invaded by pests almost overnight. A good magnifying glass will help you locate insects like scale, and there are insecticides you can use safely indoors in the winter. Read the labels carefully.

You must keep your plants clean, and that can be hard in

the winter when the house is closed up. Take a damp cloth and wipe them off, give them a shower or even wash them with a safe soap and water; rinse well.

Because winter days are shorter and the light weaker, many plants like to rest from October through May. Let them do it. Feeding them fertilizer in the winter will only make them grow spindly.

This, of course, refers only to foliage houseplants. Those that bloom, like African violets, need to be fed regularly. Pay attention to the top soil. If it's too compact, take a fork and stir carefully and not too deeply. If it's crusty and white on top, you're getting too much mineral salt because the pot isn't draining properly. Check the drainage and rinse water through the plant. If the roots push out the bottom or are matted against the side of the pot, it probably needs repotting.

You never water houseplants on a regular basis, like once a week or once a month. There are too many variables; room temperature, the plant, the type of pot, etc.

Just feel the soil. When it feels dry to the touch, soak the plant until the excess water drains away. Never let the plant sit in water. That causes root rot. When the plant dries, water it again.

Houseplants like temperatures about 70 degrees in the day and 55 to 60 at night. Don't we all. Keep the plant away from drafts and heat radiators. At the Wiche house we like to use rubber trays filled with pebbles, which we water regularly to add humidity.

Keep in mind that all plants shed leaves occasionally, especially when they are moved. Some plants — like the popular weeping fig — hate to be moved; find a spot with good light and leave it there.

Winter

NOTES

FEBRUARY

FEBRUARY CHECKLIST

EARLY

☐ Order seeds, shrubs and trees from catalogs.
☐ Throw the groundhog a party to keep him above ground.
☐ Let sun melt ice on landscape plants.
☐ Try growing some plants in low-light areas.

MIDDLE

☐ Preserve the fresh-cut flowers you received for Valentine's Day.
☐ Fertilize fruit trees.
☐ Take soil sample for testing.
☐ Start broccoli, cabbage and cauliflower indoors.

LATE

☐ Begin dormant-spray program on trees, shrubs and roses.
☐ Check stored winter bulbs for rot.
☐ Begin fertilizing some houseplants.
☐ Apply pre-emergent crab-grass killer.
☐ Fertilize woody plants and bushes before new growth begins.
☐ Remove old asparagus and rhubarb tops and side-dress plants with ammonium nitrate.
☐ Clean out dead raspberry bushes.
☐ Begin pruning fruit trees.
☐ Fertilize spring bulbs as soon as they emerge from the soil.
☐ Check houseplants for spider mites.
☐ Sneak peas into the ground.
☐ Prune deciduous landscape plants.
☐ Prune grapes.

SUPER TIP

☐ Picking the perfect time to plant.

February may really be the cruelest month, that terrible 28- or 29-day interval between the time when it's way too cold to think about gardening and the time when you can begin "mudding in" peas or starting some spinach under clear plastic.

February comes from the Latin word **februare**, which means to purify. February was once the last month of the year, and those wild and crazy Romans used to purify themselves during February to get ready for the festivals in the coming year. February was made the second month in the calendar in 46 B.C. by Julius Caesar, who could do that kind of stuff.

The average high temperature in February is 45 degrees, and the average low is 26.8 degrees. The average precipitation in Kentuckiana in February is 3.23 inches, which includes melted snowfall. Ten inches of snow equals one inch of rain.

The warmest February day in Kentuckiana occurred on Feb. 10, 1932, when the temperature hit 78 degrees. The coldest was minus 19 on Feb. 2, 1951. The coldest temperature ever in Indiana was 35 below zero in Greensburg on Feb. 7, 1951.

The most Louisville-area precipitation was the 9.84 inches that fell in 1884; the least was .40 inches in 1947. Normal snowfall for the month is 4.7 inches.

There are 10 hours and 18 minutes of sunlight on Feb. 1, which increases to 11 hours and 20 minutes by the end of the month. The soil temperature in the area — taken at four inches below sod cover — ranges from 35 to 43 degrees.

Abraham Lincoln, Charles Lindberg and Ronald Reagan were born in February.

EARLY

If you didn't order your seeds, shrubs or trees from the mail-order catalog — and don't worry, they won't be shipped until you can plant them — you better finish the job. It's getting close to planting time.

Oh yeah; don't forget to include the shipping charges in your check; millions of us forget that every year. And don't order anything that can't survive in hardiness zone 5. Most of this area is actually in zone 6 — an area south of zone 5 — but it pays to be safe.

If this is the year you're going to order strawberries — after all those years of driving to someone else's patch to pick them — you better get to it. Spring is the best season to plant them.

Do everything you can to be sure the groundhog doesn't pop back underground for another six weeks of winter. Bake him a cake, throw a party or promise him a heated dog house. Let's keep that rascal above ground after Feb. 2.

Don't try to remove ice from landscape plants. Maybe you can slip some support beneath them, but let the sun melt the ice. That will prevent broken limbs.

I'm often asked this time of year about plants that will grow in low-light areas. There are plants that do especially well in homes with north-facing windows or with big shade trees out front.

The highest on my list is the Chinese evergreen. We have two varieties, and I think it's a very attractive plant that is badly underrated. You can also try the cast-iron plant, the vining pothos, the philodendron, the snake plant and last, but never least, the mother-in-law's tongue.

If you can't grow that, stick to plastic.

MIDDLE

Let's hope you received a bouquet of flowers for Valentine's Day. Let's hope they last at least as long as the thought behind them. Here's the way to make them last:

Flower stems that are not already in the water should be recut with a sharp knife as soon as they arrive. Remove at least a half-inch of stem so the flowers can better absorb water.

Remove any excess foliage that will be underwater. Use warm water; it will move more quickly into the flower. But let the flowers sit in tepid water for 20 minutes prior to arranging them. Roses are an exception; they prefer waiting in cold water before going in the warmer vase.

Use a commercial flower food or preservative in the water. It contains sugar, acidifiers and a mild fungicide.

Avoid placing the flowers in excessive heat, such as in sunlight or on the television set. Place most flowers in a cool area — even the refrigerator — at

night. Gladioluses and orchids should not be exposed to temperatures below 50 degrees. Happy Valentine's Day.

February is the month you want to fertilize fruit trees. Fruit trees should not be fertilized in late spring or early summer because that will prompt new growth that won't mature before frost.

For apple trees, apply 1/4 pound of ammonium nitrate for each year of the tree's age; for example, use one pound around a 4-year-old tree.

For peaches, plums and cherries, use 1/6 pound of ammonium nitrate per year, and for pears use 1/8 pound. Apply the fertilizer at the drip line of the tree (the outer reach of the lower branches), because roots will grow that far away from the trunk. Throwing fertilizer against the tree trunk is mostly a waste. Water the fertilizer in if nature doesn't quickly oblige.

You can also fertilize your other trees, using a high nitrogen mix like 27-3-3. But this is not mandatory. If you fertilized your lawn twice in the fall with a high-nitrogen fertilizer, your trees may not need much more. Check their health and see.

What's this? You still haven't taken a soil sample after years of being preached to about it? Get started now. Go to your local agriculture extension office and pick up your soil bags and instructions.

Remember: You may need to take several samples. If you want to plant rhododendrons or azaleas, they'll need an acid soil that won't do in the garden. Decide what plants you want where and learn their characteristics, then work on the soil samples. Spring is the best time to plant azaleas and rhododendron, as well as evergreens, because they lose so much water through their leaves during the winter.

It's time, believe it or not, to prepare for planting cool-weather seedlings such as broccoli, cabbage and cauliflower indoors. They can be started any time from mid-February to early March.

But hold off on starting warm-weather plants such as tomatoes and green peppers. They don't go outdoors until early May, and if you begin them now, they'll get too big and leggy on you before you can get them outside — unless you have a well-equipped greenhouse.

Starting seedlings indoors can be very satisfying, but it takes a little work. To begin, find containers that will hold soil but drain easily. A milk container will do, or you can buy regular potting flats at the nursery.

Potting soil will work, but I prefer to use man-made soils like Jiffy-Mix or Ready-Earth. Fill the container with the planting medium, soak thoroughly and let it drain overnight.

Wet it again the next day, let it drain, sow your seeds ON TOP of the soil, then cover them with 1/16 inch of milled sphagnum moss.

Use a mister to soak the moss, let it drain again, then put the container in a clear plastic bag. Tie the end and put the contain-

er in a warm place, but not in direct sun.

It will take 24 for 36 hours for cole crops to sprout and five to 10 days for tomatoes or peppers. As soon as they do, remove the plastic bag and give them light and steady warmth. A window rarely works because the light is insufficient, and you will get thin, leggy plants.

The best light would be a bank of cool-white fluorescent tubes placed four to six inches above the seedlings. Move them up as the plants grow.

Keep the soil moist. In about 10 days, when the true leaves develop, feed them some fish-emulsion fertilizer. As they get bigger, transfer them into individual Styrofoam cups. In about six weeks, move the plants outdoors gradually to harden them off. Plant them neck deep in the garden when they do get outside for good.

LATE

Contrary to what you might think, it's not too early to begin your dormant-spray program on outdoor trees, shrubs and roses. It's one of the most important things you can do for them all year.

Dormant oils coat the branches and trunks with a film that suffocates the aphids, mites and scale that spent the winter clinging to fruit and ornamental plants.

BE SURE to read the label carefully and apply only as directed. Also, be sure the temperature will be above freezing for at least 24 hours after the spray is applied, or it will not work.

Dormant oil shouldn't be used on everything, which is why you must read the label. For instance, it shouldn't be used on maples and could fade the blue color of your spruce.

University of Kentucky entomologist Dr. Rudy Scheibner reminds us that dormant oil is one of the safest sprays we use and can be used any time before new growth appears.

A dormant spray of lime sulphur diluted with water is also the best way to head off blackspot disease on your roses. It's available at any gardening center.

Keep checking those stored winter bulbs for rot.

If your houseplants show signs of coming out of their winter doldrums, you might want to begin adding a little fertilizer to their water. In general, though, don't fertilize foliage houseplants until April. Also, keep picking off dead-looking leaves to encourage new growth.

Keep an eye on your forsythia bush, or maybe your neighbor's forsythia bush. It blooms just about the time you want to apply pre-emergent crab-grass killer to your lawn — sometime in late February to early March. Apply it a second time in May. You'll be so glad you applied it by July and August, when the crab grass normally attacks. But the pre-emergent needs rainfall or a good watering to get it into the soil. On many dry years it just sits there, and the crabgrass grows anyway, thumbing its nose on the way past.

You can fertilize your woody plants and bushes with a high-nitrogen fertilizer before new growth begins but after soil temperatures hit 40 degrees. You can check the temperatures with a soil thermometer or listen to agriculture reports.

If you haven't already done it, be sure to remove old asparagus and rhubarb tops and side-dress the plants with ammonium nitrate. Be sure to clean out the dead raspberry bushes if you didn't get to them last fall.

You can begin pruning fruit trees late in February. Start with the apples and leave the others until next month. When pruning apple trees, leave one strong leader or stem. Prune off competing upright limbs at the top of the tree. Then select three or four strong horizontal branches to save. Be sure they are evenly spaced around the trunk but not originating at the same level.

Fertilize spring bulbs as soon as they begin to emerge from the soil. Use a bulb-booster fertilizer or a 10-10-10 if you want to keep it simple. Don't worry about frost harming the bulbs.

PRUNING FRUIT TREES

APPLE
(Central Leader Training)

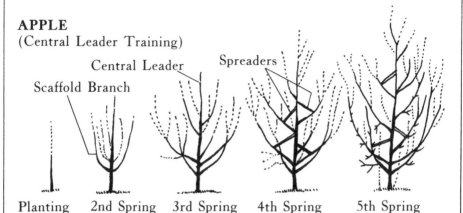

Central Leader   Spreaders

Scaffold Branch

Planting   2nd Spring   3rd Spring   4th Spring   5th Spring

(Dotted lines indicate branches to be removed)

PEAR, CHERRY & PLUM
(Modified Central Leader Training)

Planting   3rd Spring

2nd Spring   4th Spring   5th Spring

(Dotted lines indicate branches to be removed)

PEACH & NECTARINE
(Open Vase Training)

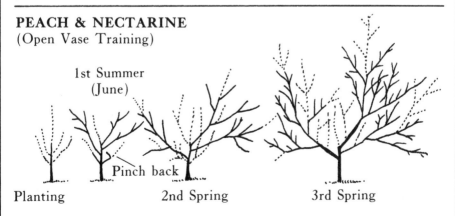

1st Summer
(June)

Pinch back

Planting   2nd Spring   3rd Spring

(Dotted lines indicate branches to be removed)

They are plenty hardy.

Double-check your houseplants for spider mites. Look for pale leaves and a very fine webbing encasing them. Wash the plants in lukewarm water or with insecticidal soap if it's a problem.

You can sneak your early peas into the ground in very late February. If you get a late start, however, you can jump-start the process by putting them in a plastic bag filled with wet sphagnum moss. Place it out of the sun but in a warm place, and in 24 hours they'll germinate, giving you a chance to catch up on a late planting.

You can also place some spinach seeds directly outdoors under a sheet of clear plastic to start them.

You can also prune your deciduous landscape plants now, but be sure you don't prune those that bloom in the spring such as forsythia, spirea and crab apple. Prune those right after the flowers fade.

Mid to late spring is the time to prune your grapes. It's not a terribly difficult task, but it must be done right if you want a decent grape crop every year. You'll be pruning off about 90 percent of last year's vines to get ready for this year.

PRUNING GRAPEVINES

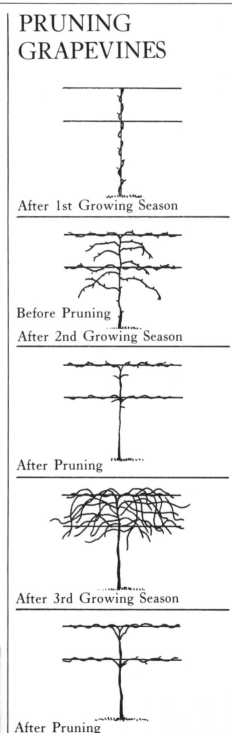

After 1st Growing Season

Before Pruning
After 2nd Growing Season

After Pruning

After 3rd Growing Season

After Pruning

FRED'S TIPS

If you're going to plant strawberries this year, consider using a pre-emergent weedkiller like Dacthal, which will help control weeds. It can be applied immediately after planting or any time during the first season if you're not going to eat the berries. Dacthal works well on many fruits and flowers, including the iris, which always causes weeding problems. You can use Dacthal now, but please, please read the label; it might injure some other crops.

Bill Young, a friend of mine who has worked for years in the agriculture and horticulture chemical industry, put it best: "We don't put labels on boxes, bags and bottles of chemicals for decoration — they are there to protect your health, as well as the health of your plants."

When you order trees and shrubs by mail, you might be surprised to learn that many come bare-rooted — without a hint of dirt on the roots. That's fine, as long as the plants are dormant. If you can't plant them right away, dig a trench and cover the roots until you can.

Twenty-four hours before planting, soak the roots of bare-root trees or bushes and plant directly into the hole. Spread out the roots. Don't be afraid to prune off the broken or injured roots.

When planning your garden, you should rotate your five main crop groups from year to year to help disease control. The groups are the nightshade family, which includes potatoes, tomatoes, eggplant and peppers. The second group is vine crops, such as cucumbers and melons. The third is corn and green manure crops, such as rye and wheat. The fourth is crucifers, such as cabbage, broccoli and cauliflower. The fifth is legumes, such as peas, along with beets and carrots.

If you have a deciduous hedge, like a privet, that's gotten too tall and scraggly due to improper pruning, it should be cut down to about six inches so it can start over again. Once the hedge has been cut back, fertilize it with a 10-10-10 mix; two to four pounds per 100 square feet. Next time prune it right; be sure the top is narrower than the bottom so the sun can get to it.

Avoid blowing or shoveling snow onto your plants. Snow, especially heavy, wet spring snow, can smash them. If there's no where else for the snow to go, wrap the plants in burlap to help them stand up.

Here's the best way to tell if your plant is pot-bound. Place one hand over the top of the pot, fingers around the stem to hold the soil in place. Invert the plant and tap the pot against the edge of the table. If the soil ball that emerges shows a thickly matted mass of roots, it's time to repot. Make sure your new pot is an inch or two larger than the old. Gently pry the root mass apart before replanting, trimming away excess roots as you go.

You would think if we could put a man on the moon we could do something about moles here on earth. But despite all the home remedies we see and read about, the best way to rid your yard of moles is with mechanical traps available at most hardware and large garden stores.

But first you've got to study the mole runs to see where they are working the hardest and check your traps religiously.

Killing lawn grubs with insecticides can help, but moles also eat earthworms. Those with time and patience can watch the mole runs for signs of activity, then "eliminate" the pests with a spade or shovel. Or try paying the neighborhood kid $5 a mole; it might be cheaper.

Good luck.

Horse or cow manure can make a great compost, especially when mixed with straw or sawdust. But for best results let it sit under black plastic for a year to kill the weeds and to let the manure settle out. The ammonia in fresh manure can kill a plant.

Here are a dozen trees the University of Kentucky says should not be planted in the urban home landscape because they are either too weak, have invasive roots, produce messy fruit or have too many suckers: catalpa, silver maple, mulberry, Lombardy poplar, tree of heaven, osage orange, box elder, European white birch, cottonwood, black locust, Siberian elm and willows.

FRED'S SUPER TIP

You will notice that the information at the beginning of each chapter includes average soil temperatures for the month around Kentuckiana. Those figures will fluctuate every year and are only intended as general indicators.

Ground temperatures, like air temperatures, can fluctuate as much as 20 to 30 degrees a day near the surface. But as you go 20 inches underground, the temperature may fluctuate only one degree in a day.

In most years, the average soil temperature is the lowest in mid-January and early February; often in the mid 30s. It's warmest in late July and early August, often in the low 80s.

Official Kentucky ground temperatures are taken four inches below sod, which provides a constant all tracking stations use. The bare soil in your garden, of course, will be several degrees warmer than it is four inches below sod.

It's important to know this because many plants have minimum temperatures below which seeds will not germinate. In a particularly cold, wet spring, the seed could rot.

Although the time when the soil reaches a certain optimum temperature may vary from year to year, the annual cycle is usually consistent. Heavy rains and wet soil may delay the warming, but rarely by more than one or two weeks.

So it pays to keep track of soil temperatures, either with a thermometer or by monitoring farm reports. For instance, it's known that the minimum temperature for corn germination is about 50 degrees, but germination would be very slow at that temperature. The optimum is 60 degrees and above, but when the temperature hits 107 — not unusual in a bare field in midsummer — it's too hot for germination.

Tomato sets make their best growth when soil temperatures hit 85 degrees, an easy temperature to find during a summer day, although it may drop below that at night. Tomato growth is very slow at 55 to 60 degrees.

So here then is a brief list of the MINIMUM temperatures needed for the following vegetables to germinate; asparagus, 50 degrees; beets, 40 degrees; cabbage, 40 degrees; carrots, 40 degrees; cucumbers, 60 degrees; lettuce, 35 degrees; onions, 35 degrees; peas, 40 degrees; radishes, 40 degrees; squash, 60 degrees; melons, 60 degrees.

Knowing that should help with planting.

NOTES

MARCH

MARCH CHECKLIST

EARLY
- ☐ Force forsythia and pussy willow to bloom indoors.
- ☐ Plan vegetable and flower gardens.
- ☐ Prepare soil near house for small salad garden.
- ☐ Sharpen shears and checks rakes and hoes.
- ☐ Plant rhubarb.

MIDDLE
- ☐ Plant cool-season crops such as cabbage, brussels sprouts, turnips, peas, carrots, lettuce, cauliflower, broccoli, kohlrabi and collards.
- ☐ Examine transplants for disease.
- ☐ Protect transplants from cutworms.
- ☐ Transplant cool-season flowers outdoors.
- ☐ Finish spraying fruit trees and berry plants with dormant oil.
- ☐ Examine leftover pesticides for signs of age or damage.
- ☐ Apply pre-emergent herbicides to flower beds and vegetable garden.
- ☐ Plant asparagus.

LATE
- ☐ Remove flower stalks from spring-flowering plants and fertilize beds.
- ☐ Cut back liriope before new growth begins.
- ☐ Divide perennials and plant new ones.
- ☐ Fertilize houseplants every other week.
- ☐ Start caladiums indoors.
- ☐ Spray pine trees suffering from scale.

SUPER TIP
- ☐ Think small when planting fruit trees.

March is the time when winter finally melts into the magic of springtime bulbs, high school basketball turns into March Madness, and the NCAA playoffs begin. What could be better than that?

March is named for Mars, the Roman god of war, who probably tore up a lot of gardens in his day.

The average high temperature is 54.9 degrees, and the average low is 35.2, with plenty of nasty freezes left, so don't get in too big a hurry to plant.

The average March precipitation is 4.73 inches, but sometimes that all comes at once. Some 14.97 inches of precipitation fell in March 1964, including a gully-washing 6.97 inches on March 9, producing what's lovingly known as the '64 Flood. The least precipitation ever in March was in 1930 when only .12 inches fell.

The highest temperature ever in March was 88 degrees, which occurred twice: March 22, 1907 and March 25, 1929. The coldest was a nose-tweeking 1 degree below zero on March 6, 1960, which must have surprised a lot of potatoes.

March, 1960 was a dandy. It produced 18 inches of snow in Bowling Green on March 9, the state record for one day. It dumped 46.5 inches of snow on Benham in Harlan County, a state record for one month. Poor Benham had 96.7 inches of snow that year. As comparison, the normal snow in Louisville for March is 3.9 inches.

There are 11 hours and 21 minutes of possible sunlight on March 1, but we rarely get that much. By March 31 the sun is up 12 hours and 35 minutes.

The average soil temperature — at a depth of four inches below sod — ranges from 45 to 52 degrees.

Knute Rockne, the famous Notre Dame football coach with the "golden thumb," was born March 4, 1888. Julius Caesar, the man who could move months, was assassinated March 15, 44 B.C. — so beware the Ides of March.

EARLY

Although they'll be blooming outdoors any time, you can still "force" forsythia or pussy willow to bloom indoors. Go out to the bush, snip off a few extraneous limbs, then place the cuttings in warm water. In a few days you'll have a little touch of spring blossoming in your house.

If you haven't planned your vegetable or flower gardens, it's past time to get started. Draw up a rough plan of what you want, being sure to rotate crops to a different spot from where they were last year. Remember, smaller plants should be grown in front of the taller ones so they will have sufficient sunlight. For vegetables, that's at least six hours a day.

If you want a small area near the house in which to begin a salad garden, you can lay a sheet of clear plastic on the ground and hold it down with bricks.

That will warm and dry the soil, giving you a head start.

But don't be overanxious to plant. Test the soil by squeezing it with one hand. If it crumbles and slips through your fingers, the soil is ready to work. If it wads up like a ball of putty, it's still too early to plant.

Pruning season means you must have sharp tools. A well-sharpened pair of shears should cut through a facial tissue or a single sheet of newspaper. If your shears aren't that sharp, find a good sharpening service and get them honed. You'll be glad you did, and so will your plants. Check the condition of your rakes, shovels and hoes while in the garage.

If you have your heart set on rhubarb-strawberry pie, early to mid-March is the best time to plant the rhubarb part of that delicious combination.

Rhubarb thrives in a sunny location in fertile, well-prepared soil. Work the soil as soon as you can. Incorporate peat moss, compost or well-rotted manure. Set the new plants (crown and bud side up) three to four inches deep and about three to four feet apart. Water deeply during dry spells and fertilize in midsummer and early each spring.

Do not harvest any rhubarb the year you plant it. Starting the second year, you can harvest for about six weeks in spring and early summer. Grab the large outer stalks near their base and twist them off. Do not pull more than two-thirds of the stalks off any plant. Throw away all leaves because the foliage is poisonous.

MIDDLE

Mid-March is the time to plant cool-season crops such as cabbage, brussels sprouts, turnips, peas, carrots, lettuce, cauliflower, broccoli, kohlrabi and collards.

For best results, cabbage, brussels sprouts, cauliflower and broccoli should be grown from transplants. The others can be grown from seeds.

Examine the transplants for disease before planting. Look for galls, ash-gray leaf spots and cankers. Discard any that look sickly. The best transplants are often the stocky ones with the thick stems.

Cabbage and other cole crops are susceptible to cutworms, which are often found in gardens where there had been grass the year before. Cutworms literally cut the plants off at the ground line and don't even bother to holler "timmmberrrr."

Paper collars wrapped around the plants' stems will prevent cutworm damage, or you can buy cutworm bait at a seed store. Diazinon powder that you wet may be used on the soil prior to setting out transplants to protect them against cutworms and root maggots.

Although we don't often think of flowers in March, cool-season flowers such as snapdragons, pansies, ornamental cabbage, dwarf carnations, pinks, primrose and sweet williams should be transplanted outdoors during mid- to late March, with March 20 considered about the best time most years. These flowers will need at least five hours of sun a day and are tough enough to sustain a light frost.

You are running out of time to effectively spray fruit trees and raspberry plants with dormant oil to protect them against diseases like peach-leaf curl, plum pockets and anthracnose.

You'll find more complete information on spraying with dormant oil in the February chapter, but that's only the first job in what can be a season-long battle against bugs and diseases.

If you are serious about raising good fruits and berries, contact the nearest Kentucky Cooperative Extension Service office and ask for a copy of brochure ID-21, "Pest Control Program for Home-Grown Fruit in Kentucky." It does a much better job of explaining the complex spraying program than I can in a limited space. Persons living in other states should get a similiar brochure from their state ag agents.

Pesticides purchased last year, or pesticides that were stored in the garage over the winter, should be examined for signs of age or damage.

Sludge-like material at the bottom, cracks in the containers, bulges in the sides and strong odors are indicators the pesticides have been damaged. If all indications are bad, the pesticide should be thrown out. The Environmental Protection Agency says wrap them deep in newspapers and discard them in the garbage.

Perhaps one of the most important steps you can take in mid-March is to kill weed seeds as they germinate by working pre-emergent herbicides into the soil as you prepare the beds.

Both Treflan and Dacthal are suitable for use in flower beds and the vegetable garden. Be absolutely sure to use only as directed on the label. Also, remember that a pre-emergent cannot be used in all parts of a vegetable garden. Some crops, such as corn, can be damaged by pre-emergent herbicides, so you'll have to leave an untreated area for some vegetables.

Asparagus, like rhubarb, can be planted in mid-March. It grows best in full sun, maybe at the north or west side of your garden where it won't be disturbed or shaded by vegetables. Also, keep in mind that it will grow four to six feet high and would make a nice screen. It also grows well along a fence.

Asparagus must have well-drained soil. Dig a trench 12 inches deep and 15 inches wide. Add generous amounts of compost, peat moss and well-rotted manure to a depth of about 6 inches. Then add about 1/4 cup of 5-20-20 fertilizer per plant.

Plant roots that are one year old, allowing a dozen for each member of your family. Set the roots at the bottom of the trench, which is now about six inches deep; the plants should be about 18 inches apart. Be sure the crowns are facing up. Cover the roots with three to four inches of soil but not all the way to ground level. Then fill in the trench gradually as the shoots grow, always leaving the tips exposed. Every fall, after the top growth is cut back, mulch over the top of the bed. This eventually produces a long ridge.

New research indicates that some light cutting can be made for about four weeks the spring after planting. In the second year, a normal eight-week cutting period can be started.

LATE

After the blossoms of spring-flowering bulbs have faded, cut off the spent flower stalks, then feed the plants with 1/2 cup of 5-10-10 fertilizer per 10 square feet of bed if you didn't do it earlier. The best time to feed the bulbs is when the foliage is breaking through the ground.

Do not remove the foliage after the flower fades; it's needed to replenish the underground bulb. Once the foliage begins to yellow naturally, it's fine to remove it.

You can rejuvenate your liriope (monkey grass) by using a lawn mower to cut back the old foliage to 3 or 4 inches. This should be done before new growth begins. If your plant has started new growth, be sure to cut above it.

If you didn't get to divide your perennials last fall, or you'd like to plant more, there's still time. Choices for sunny areas include day lilies, yarrow, Shasta daisies, perennial phlox and coneflowers. Shade-loving perennials include columbines, hostas and ferns.

As warmer weather approaches, it's time to think about feeding your houseplants every other week with a water-soluble fertilizer like 18-18-18 or 20-20-20. A lot depends on the weather, but late March to April is the time to wake up your houseplants and get them ready to be moved outside.

While you're waking things up, caladiums, which produce marvelously showy leaves all summer, are best started indoors to get their engines running. Start them in flats or pots that are at least 30 percent sphagnum moss or compost. Plant the tubers about an inch deep in bright, indirect light. Keep them moist. When the outdoor soil temperature is about 60 degrees, move them outdoors. To encourage fuller growth, remove the center tuber as it develops.

If your pine trees have taken on a different color, looking almost a ghostly white, it isn't paint; it's an insect called scale. Scale is especially bad on low-growing pines. It spends the winter under those white spots, then emerges in spring to suck vital juices from the needles. It can be controlled with a lime-sulphur dormant spray applied when temperatures are above freezing for 24 hours. Later in the summer an insecticide like Orthene or

Isotox will control scale.

FRED'S TIPS

A few years ago I received a great tip from a Mount Washington, Ky., woman for protecting baby plants during cold weather. She said that as she sets out broccoli, cauliflower and brussels sprouts, she covers each plant with a paper cup with the bottom cut out. On extra-cold nights, she covers that cup with another cup with the bottom left in it. The first cup allows sun through the top. The second keeps out the cold.

March is a good time to bath houseplants in hot water to get them ready to go outdoors in the spring. Begin by filling a sink or tub with liquid or flake soap; don't use detergent because it is too strong. Put the pot in a plastic bag, drawing the top of the bag around the base of the plant so the dirt doesn't spill into the sink.

Turn the container upside down and swish the foliage around in the soapy water. If you think spider mites have attacked your plant, don't rinse the leaves; the soap provides some protection. If there are no insects, go ahead and rinse the plant. Most plants, with the exception of fuzzy-leafed varieties such as African violets, or ferns, cactus and succulents, like a bath three or four times a year.

If you have shady areas in your yard but still want some colorful understory trees in those areas, consider the dogwood, redbud and Canadian or Carolina hemlock. For shrubs, consider the glossy abelia, Oregon grape holly or witch hazel. All plants need some light to grow, but these will tolerate shade as long as it isn't as dark as the inside of a closet.

I get a lot of complaints in the spring about moss growing under trees such as maples or in any area of the lawn that is shady, damp and has poor air circulation. Spreading lime helps a little, but there's really not too much that can be done about moss except to rake it up. You might try a shade-tolerating grass such as fescue or rye, but the best answer is a ground cover such as ivy, pachysandra, vinca minor or ajuga.

The roots of a walnut tree give off a toxic material that is injurious to many plants. Try a raised-bed garden in those areas, but only if you plant shallow-rooted plants such as lettuce and impatiens that also tolerate shade. Deep-rooted plants may come in contact with walnut roots. Also, remember that a raised bed that is too big might injure tree roots.

A sun box made of aluminum foil can brighten your prospects for growing straight and sturdy transplants indoors when the sun is scarce.

Set plants in a large cardboard box with the front cut out and the back lined with aluminum foil. When placed near windows, the foil lining reflects the light back onto the plants, and stems grow straight instead of leaning toward the sun.

The sun box is reusable year after year. Leftover aluminum strips can be placed at the base of squash plants where the reflected light will discourage bugs that like to lay eggs in the normally dark stem area. Aluminum foil placed around a garden has also been known to discourage night-prowling bunnies.

The carrot is another vegetable that will benefit from having seeds soaked in water for a few hours before planting. One year, on the advice of a friend, I poured the carrot seeds into a sprinkling can, then walked up and down a row sprinkling and sowing at the same time.

After several days, when nothing came up, I told my friend his idea didn't work. He told me to take the nozzle off my can.

I did. There were the seeds. If you try this, be sure the holes in the can are large enough to allow the seeds to pass through.

When cutting up seed potatoes before planting, it's best to let them heal for about 24 hours so the pieces can "scar" over. Be sure to get at least one eye in each piece or the potato will never see its way to the top.

Get them in as early as possible. You can bury them about six inches deep and a few feet apart, although some people have had great luck growing potatoes under nothing but a straw mulch. Even if you bury them, straw mulch is a good idea.

The insecticide Thiodan has been successful against the dreaded Colorado potato beetle in recent years, but the beetles are now showing signs of becoming immune to that. What's a gardener to do.

If you're just beginning to garden and are in need of some "sure-thing" annual flowers, the specialists at the University of Kentucky say begonias, periwinkles, ornamental peppers, impatiens and coleus do best in the Kentuckiana climate. All do well in the garden or in containers.

In the absence of a soil test, you can get by in your garden by applying 25 pounds of 5-10-10 or 6-12-12 fertilizer per 1,000 square feet of gardening area. That's about 2 1/2 pounds per 100 square feet. Add two tablespoons of 5-10-10 fertilizer or 6-12-12 per bushel of soil for container growing.

Early spring, after the serious frost has departed but before the temperatures rise into the 50s and 60s, is the best time to prune grapes. There are several ways of doing this depending on space and variety.

The best advice I can give is to find a publication showing how a properly pruned grape arbor should look. Your local extension service or garden-supply store should have it. This is very important because about 90 percent of a grape arbor is pruned each year, and you have to know which 90 percent.

FRED'S SUPER TIP

If you are thinking about adding fruit trees to your garden this year, let me give you one piece of advice: Think small.

There's room in almost every home garden for dwarf or semi-dwarf apple trees; be sure to buy at least two or they'll not pollinate. Not only do these trees require less space, but they can be pruned, thinned, sprayed and harvested from the ground or with the use of a small ladder. They may cost more initially, but they will save money in the long run.

When it comes to cherry trees, all we have in our garden is "Northstar Dwarf" and "Montmorence Dwarf." I would never have a standard cherry tree because the birds get most of the harvest. Our trees are only seven to eight feet tall, and when the cherries ripen we can cover them with fruit-tree netting and get our full harvest. If you're thinking about cherry trees, buy only tart; sweet cherries will rarely develop a crop in this part of the country.

Fruit trees should be fertilized now, not in late spring or summer. An apple tree requires 1/4 pound of ammonium nitrate for each year of the tree's age. Peaches, plums and cherries use 1/6 pound for each year, and pears use 1/8 pound. Spread the fertilizer below the drip line of the tree, not up against the trunk.

One final thought on trees: Spend a little money and buy the most disease-resistant varieties available. I don't have to spray them with fungicides all summer. Among apple trees, the disease-resistant would include Liberty, Freedom, Prima, Priscilla, Jonafree and Redfree.

NOTES

APRIL

APRIL CHECKLIST

EARLY

- ☐ Start warm-weather crops indoors.
- ☐ Repair the lawn.
- ☐ Consider Zoysia and Bermuda grasses.
- ☐ Fertilize, prune and spray rose bushes.
- ☐ Check tulip bed for tulip fire disease.
- ☐ Plant carrots and radishes.
- ☐ Check tubers and corms of gladioluses and cannas.
- ☐ Start tuberous begonias indoors.
- ☐ Apply weedkiller to wild garlic.
- ☐ Take wrapping off trees planted last fall.
- ☐ Plant new trees.

MIDDLE

- ☐ Plant snap and lima beans.
- ☐ Prune spring-flowering shrubs after blooms fade.
- ☐ Start transplants for muskmelon and watermelon.
- ☐ Check strawberry plants.
- ☐ Fertilize magnolias.
- ☐ Prune peach trees.
- ☐ Fertilize trees.

LATE

- ☐ Check vegetable garden for aphids.
- ☐ Protect vegetable garden from rabbits.
- ☐ Blanch cauliflower.
- ☐ Apply weedkiller to dandelions.
- ☐ Prune peony buds.
- ☐ Fertilize evergreens.
- ☐ Check trees for tent caterpillars.

SUPER TIP

- ☐ How to start seeds in a bag.

April is the month we've all been waiting for. The tulips are up and hoping to make it to Derby Week — and so are we. But caution is advised. Although the last average frost date in this area is in early April, that varies greatly from year to year, and it's still too early to plant the more sensitive plants.

April apparently takes its name from the Latin word **aperire**, which means "to open." There is another school of thought that says it was named for Aphrodite, the Greek goddess of love, and that makes sense too.

The average high temperature in April is 67.5 degrees; the average low is 45.6 degrees. The average precipitation is 4.11 inches, which means more rain normally falls in March, even if we think of April showers in song and story.

A record 11.10 inches of rain fell in Louisville in March 1970. (They started keeping records in the 1870s.) The least-ever April rain was .25 inches in 1896, a good spring for dry humor.

The warmest April day ever was April 23, 1925, and April 24, 1960, when the temperature hit 91 degrees. The coldest day was April 18, 1875, when it was 21 degrees, and that must have tested some peach crops.

The average snowfall in the Louisville area for April — a statistic that rarely wears out the weatherman's pencil — is .2 inches.

There are 12 hours and 37 minutes of possible sunlight on April 1, and 13 hours and 45 minutes by April 30. The average soil temperature ranges between 52 and 59 degrees.

The Indian Pocahontas, who had something to do with home-grown Thanksgiving dishes, married John Rolfe on April 5, 1614, and the Pony Express began on April 3, 1860, probably to deliver seed catalogs.

EARLY

If you want to start flowers or warm-season vegetables like tomatoes, peppers and eggplant indoors to get them ready for planting outdoors in May, April 1 is a good day to begin.

Plant the seeds in a container of good, sterile potting soil. After the container has been thoroughly soaked, sprinkle the top of the growing medium with milled sphagnum moss. Often when the little seedlings are breaking through the soil they are hit with a disease called "damping off," but I've never had that happen with a 1/8-inch thick layer of milled sphagnum.

Next, place the container in a clear plastic bag and seal the end, creating a miniature greenhouse. Another trick I use is to place the bag in front of a floor heat register or at the foot of the refrigerator. That will provide enough heat.

If you place the bag in the sun, you might end up with prematurely cooked vegetables. One hazard of placing the bag in front of the refrigerator, however, is that sometimes you end up with depressions that look suspiciously like a dropped package of frozen hot dogs.

Watch the seeds closely. As soon as the tiny plants poke their heads through the soil and begin looking around, place them about three to four inches below a bank of fluorescent lights. Government studies, and my experience, have shown that regular cool, white fluorescent lights are just as effective in starting plants as the more expensive grow lights.

But if you like the distinctive color the grow lights give your plants, try mixing one plain fluorescent tube and one grow light in your white enamel fixture.

Fall is considered the best time of the year to plant grass, but if you've got some bare patches that need work, or just can't wait that long, then early spring is the next best time.

Don't believe the old saying that you can just toss grass seed out on the snow and let it melt into the ground while you sit around reading gardening catalogs.

The seed must come in contact with bare dirt, and you're the one who has to prepare the ground. Around my Shelby County home I sow the new tall fescue varieties which seem to do better in our area than our beloved bluegrass.

Some people will even sow their entire lawns in 31-Fescue, which has a much wider, more course blade than bluegrass, and is also insect- and disease-resistant. The only thing better than 31-Fescue is green asphalt.

If you only have a few small areas of lawn that need attention, cover those bare spots with wet burlap after reseeding and keep them moist. The grass will germinate amazingly fast, so be sure to remove the burlap so the

sun can do its work. No one wants to grow feed sacks.

While we're on the subject, let's talk a little bit about the pros and cons of Zoysia and Bermuda grasses.

Zoysia grass will produce a thick, beautiful carpet of green and is almost drought-proof. During a recent drought there was a lawn of Zoysia grass in a Louisville suburb that was creating traffic problems; while every lawn around was brown and dead-looking, this one was still a bright green. People driving past were stopping, getting out of their cars and trying to grab a piece, thinking it was AstroTurf the homeowner had put down as a joke.

But — and here's the bad news — Zoysia will turn straw brown in color from the first frost of fall until the weather really warms up in May, although I do know of one Zoysia lover who uses a dye to color his lawn green for the winter.

Also, Zoysia and Bermuda grasses do not know when to quit. If your neighbor's lawn joins yours and there is not a mile-wide buffer of concrete between them, your neighbor will soon inherit your Bermuda or Zoysia, which can make for poor relationships.

Bermuda and Zoysia are also full-sun grasses. They do not like shade, which can be a problem for those of us who like trees in our lawn landscape. That's why these grasses are commonly used on golf greens, and I have never seen a tree growing on a golf-course green, although that could make for an interesting hazard.

Early April is the time to prepare the royal rose, the Queen of Flowers, for another growing season.

First remove the protective mounds of mulch you put around the roses last fall, but don't take it too far away because you may need it again for one of our spring freezes. Also, be careful not to break off some of the new basal shoots that developed beneath the mound of mulch while you were out buying Valentine's Day candy.

Once the mulch has been removed, an application of fertilizer will get the roses off and running. Monty Justice, a member of the Louisville Rose Society, recommends a liquid fertilizer supplement called Watch Us Grow combined with a teaspoon of chelated iron per gallon of water. He pours this over each rose bush at the rate of one gallon for every three square feet. He does this every seven to 10 days until four applications have been made. Be sure to water the ground well before using this treatment.

Another excellent rose gardener who was a very good friend of mine, the late "Uncle Charlie" Dawson of Simpsonville, Ky., recommended applying a tablespoon of Epsom salts per plant in the spring and then repeating the treatment 90 days later. He said this prevents leaf loss. Epsom salts are a very convenient and inexpensive form of magnesium, which helps in the manufacture of chlorophyll, the plant's "green machine."

It's still early April, so there's no big hurry to prune. You can remove the weak or rotted stems, but be sure to toss them in the trash so diseases don't hang around. If you're not sure which shoots to prune, wait another week. When pruning, make the cut at an angle just above the new shoot developing on the outside edge of last year's cane.

If you have just a few roses, you might consider putting a thumb tack in the cut ends of the canes, a trick Uncle Charlie taught me to keep the dreaded borer from sneaking into the tips.

It's also time to begin your spray program of insecticides and fungicides. Extra work now will reward you with a summer rose that would have made Uncle Charlie beam with pride.

Moist early spring weather is favorable for Botrytis blight, or tulip fire disease. The disease may appear on leaves as small gray or tan oval spots having a water-soaked margin. The blight may also produce stunted, distorted and rolled leaves.

Tulip fire disease can destroy a whole tulip bed in just a few days of wet, humid weather. To prevent it, be sure the bed is in an area with good drainage, keep the bed weeded, remove and destroy old flowers and spray, if needed, with fungicides such as Zineb, Ferbam or Maneb.

DO NOT cut back the leaves of healthy plants. Let them die back naturally, because the bulb needs their help to store up food for next year's assault on your senses.

If you don't like the look of a bed full of headless tulips, interplant with summer annuals like geraniums and impatiens.

Carrots can be planted any time in early April, but getting them to germinate in cooler weather can be a problem. One way to jump-start any seeds is to soak them in water for a few hours, which can hurry germination outdoors.

Once outdoors, the biggest spring problem is the continual crusting over of the soil due to rain and baking sun. You can beat this by placing a board over the row or a piece of damp burlap which you can easily keep moist. Just remember to remove these covers as soon as the new seedlings appear, or you may hear muffled cries for help.

Another trick is to plant radish seeds with carrot seeds. The fast-germinating radishes will break up the crust, but be sure to remove some of the radishes or the carrots won't have room to grow.

Radishes are best harvested early anyway. If they get too big, they get hot, and the only thing worse than biting into a warm-weather radish is gargling with Tabasco sauce.

Now that April is here, it's time to check the tubers and corms of the gladioluses and cannas you stored last fall. You should have sprinkled a little fungicide over them when you stored them. If you spot any rotten ones, throw them away immediately. One bad tuber or corm can ruin a whole barrel of glads or cannas very quickly. Don't plant the good ones yet, however, it's much too early. They need warm weather to get started.

You can start your tuberous begonias inside now. Begin with a good soil mix of one part potting soil, one part perlite and one part organic matter. Plant the tubers in a pot with drainage holes, then tip each tuber slightly so water does not collect in the indented crowns, which must be facing up. Place your begonias in a window receiving bright sunlight to assure good growth.

This is the season for wild garlic, a tufted, obnoxious weed that looks like an onion and definitely smells like one, especially when you trim off the tops with a lawn mower.

Wild garlic can be controlled with 2-4-D weedkiller if it is applied when air temperatures reach 55 to 60 degrees for two or three days. The same chemical can also kill broadleaf weeds such as dandelions and plantain.

Always read the label and apply only as directed. For small patches of wild garlic or dandelions, I use an old plastic sprinkling can marked with a big red "X." That way I can spot-treat the lawn, applying the chemical directly to the problem area rather than spraying the whole lawn.

Since the sprinkling can is marked with a red "X," I know it can never be used for anything else. The residue from 2-4-D weedkiller will linger inside the can, and if it were used to water the garden, it would bring a quick end to the growing season.

If you planted some new trees last fall and wrapped them with protective paper, it's time to remove the wrapping and let the little guys breathe. Never leave any kind of wrap on a tree in warm weather because it is the perfect place for insects and diseases to develop.

If you're thinking about planting a new tree this spring, think about the ultimate size of the tree before you plant. That cute little pin oak planted too close to the house might be taking out your gutters in a few years.

When you decide what tree you want, find a mature specimen of that variety somewhere in your community. Stand with your back against the trunk and walk to the outer drip line, which is the outer reaches of the branches, and write down how many steps you took.

Then put a stake in the ground where you want the tree, and walk the same distance in all directions, putting additional stakes in the ground. Stand back and take a look at the area the tree will eventually occupy.

Trees are among the most valuable additions to the home landscape. They can add hundreds of dollars to the value of property — if they are planted properly.

If you ordered new trees from a catalog, chances are they will arrive bare-rooted. With these trees, or any kind of shrubs, it's best to soak the roots in cool water 24 hours before planting.

Dig the hole about 12 inches deeper and wider than the roots. The old practice was to amend the soil with sand or peat moss, but that is no longer the case. The new theory is that the soil we have here is basically clay, and if you make it nice and loamy like potting soil, the roots become weak as they grow through it. When the roots reach the clay, they are too weak to penetrate it and will grow around the side of the hole, eventually strangling the plant. This is true even if the new tree comes in a burlap ball.

When digging, put the dirt in two piles, with the top six inches in one pile and the rest in another. When planting the tree or shrub, use the top soil to fill in around the roots since it is the best. Fill the hole three-quarters full of soil, tamp gently, then fill with water and let it drain away. Then finish filling the hole, being sure the soil is not above the graft at the base of the tree. Leave a little depression around the base of the tree to catch rainwater.

Anything but burlap must be removed from around the rootball. The burlap will disintegrate. Be sure to water your new tree or shrub every week if Mother Nature does not.

Larger trees should be staked to hold roots in place.

MIDDLE

Mid- to late April is a good time to plant both snap and lima beans provided the soil is warm enough, about 45 degrees. I recommend using a soil thermometer to test the temperature; such thermometers are sold at most large gardening centers.

In addition to having the right temperature, beans can be encouraged to sprout quickly with a 30-minute bath in warm water before hitting the ground; but if it's been a particularly cool spring, you might as well wait another week, especially with the more sensitive lima beans. Even if they do sprout in cool weather, they might rot before sticking their noses up through the soil.

Also, be sure not to plant the seeds too deep. One inch is plenty. It also helps to mix a little sand with the soil to let the sprouts push up more easily, especially in clay.

Be careful not to overwater because the roots can drown easily. Light applications of fertilizer as a side-dressing will help, but go easy on the nitrogen. Especially hot weather will stop pollen growth and cause bean blossoms to drop, so all you can do is wait for the weather to change.

When it's extremely hot, I recommend using a soaker hose placed at about the drip line of the plants. The drier the foliage, the less likely they will have disease problems.

Most gardeners space rows of bush beans two to three feet apart. But one year, as an experiment, my youngest daughter, Jeneen, planted her beans in a block

about 10 feet long and four feet wide with only an inch or two between rows. She had a difficult time getting the weeds out of those narrow rows, but as the beans developed, they shaded out a lot of the weeds. The thick covering also kept the soil much moister than in my patch, where the rows were two to three feet apart.

When all was said and done, her bean block outproduced my bean rows about two to one. However, I would allow a little more room between the rows — at least three inches.

As soon as those spring-flowering shrubs have finished blooming, get out the pruning shears and get busy. Shrubs that bloom in the spring should be pruned as soon as the flowers fade, and before new growth begins.

Plants that bloom before mid-June should be pruned after they are finished blooming. They bloom on old wood, and early spring pruning would eliminate the blossoms.

Plants that bloom after mid-June can be pruned in late winter or early spring because they bloom on new wood — wood that is produced in mid- to late spring.

By pruning, I don't mean shear the tops off. Look down inside the shrubs and select 20 percent of the old, thickest canes and cut them off as close to the ground as you can. The more open the shrub, the better the light can penetrate down inside the shrub, promoting new growth for next year.

Acid-loving azaleas can be

pruned after blooming, but only if you really need to keep them in bounds. Azaleas look much better if they are allowed to grow naturally. Spring-flowering shrubs should be fertilized immediately after they finish blooming, and then again one month later.

Also, cut off the faded blossoms on rhododendrons. If you do, you will have many more blossoms the following year.

It is a little early to plant muskmelons and watermelons, but you can get a big jump on the season by buying transplants or starting some on your own. If you purchase them or start them yourself, be sure they are started in individual peat containers so they can be planted without disturbing their roots.

Another trick is to lay sheets of black plastic in your melon patch two to three weeks before planting to warm the soil, then cut slits in the plastic for planting.

Have you checked your strawberries yet? Be sure to remove the winter mulch when you see the strawberries start to grow and before the buds emerge from the crown. Be careful not to break off the sensitive buds. If you're thinking about planting strawberries this spring, be sure to remember to plant them so the dirt comes halfway up the crown.

If you had spittle bugs in your strawberries last year — those are tiny, yellowish-green insects that hide in balls of their own froth — apply Thiodan early. Once strawberries start to ripen, you can't use chemicals to get at the bugs.

If it's been a particularly severe winter, the leaves on your magnolia tree may look as if they've been bronzed for posterity. But remember, this is as far north as you will find the magnolia grandiflora, and such winter damage will occur every time the temperature drops to zero or below.

What to do now? Fertilize them with a fertilizer formulated for magnolias and keep them well-watered during dry periods in spring and summer. Many will come back a lot better than you think.

The pruning of peach trees in the spring should be delayed until just before bloom. To prune a peach tree remove the central leader and leave side limbs that form a little basket, or pinwheel, so sun can reach the center.

Never prune in the fall. Even mid-winter pruning can hasten plant development in the spring, which could be damaged by a late spring freeze. Apples, however, can be pruned as early as late February.

How do you check for fruit-bud damage after a tough winter? Dead buds will not swell in the spring if they are killed in the winter. If injury occurs closer to the time the fruit tree blooms, the flower center, or pistil, will be black.

In the case of apple or pear trees, you can cut across the flower and remove the top half to get a better look at the underlying tissue.

By looking at 25 to 50 buds, or flowers, you can get a rough estimate of injury.

Recent studies have shown that when peach trees reach full bloom, a temperature of 27 degrees will kill about 10 per cent of the blossoms, but 24 degrees, just a little drop, will kill 90 per cent.

Apple trees in the "full pink" stage will lose 10 per cent of the crop at 28 degrees, but 90 per cent at 25 degrees.

Tree roots begin absorbing nutrients when the soil temperature goes above 40 degrees, which often occurs in April. New research indicates that a tree's roots will extend well beyond the drip line at its outer edge — a tree 45 feet tall might have roots extending 40 feet beyond the drip line. Keep that in mind when watering and fertilizing.

The old method of boring holes to fertilize trees is no longer popular. Spread granular or liquid fertilizer over the surface of the soil. Feeder roots grow up to just an inch under the soil surface.

LATE

Henry Kirchner, one of the area's best vegetable growers, called me toward the end of April one year to warn me that the aphids had arrived.

Aphids are tiny sucking insects that multiply like ants at a picnic and seem to take over a whole plant overnight. Henry called to say that the aphids were trying to take over his cabbages and that all gardeners should look for them in the spring.

Insecticides like Malathion and Spectracide will help, but so will something else that might surprise you — aluminum foil used as a reflective mulch.

Entomologists at the U.S. Department of Agriculture's Maryland research center said using sheets of aluminum foil as a mulch will repel sucking insects like aphids that transmit viral diseases from plant to plant. The scientists said the use of aluminum foil in muskmelon plots will reduce aphids by 96 percent and also repel leaf hoppers, thrips and Mexican bean beetles.

We are now well into a new growing season, and those tender plants of peas, broccoli, cabbage and cauliflower look tempting to any rabbit in the neighborhood.

Over the years I have tried or looked at almost every method of rabbit control. Most of the methods include applying a chemical to the foliage of the plant. They don't work consistently because one rainfall will wash away all the protection.

One method I did see that worked was the use of small-hole wire called hardware cloth. The gardener made a tent-like structure out of wire as long as his row of peas, with another piece of wire stretched across each end. The tent was about eight inches high, and by the time his peas had grown that big the rabbits had found another feeding ground. The wire could be stored easily in his barn over the winter.

In smaller gardens, gallon-sized milk jugs with their bottoms cut out make perfect protective greenhouses for baby broccoli, cabbage and cauliflower plants. They will keep out the rabbits, marauding birds looking for nesting material, and — with their caps screwed on — provide frost-free homes on frosty spring mornings.

These early plants can go outdoors as soon as the ground can be worked, but frost-free protection is important because cauliflower will have a hard time recuperating from temperatures below 25 degrees, and too much cold can force broccoli to form scattered heads instead of one nice big one, but that often depends on the health of the transplants.

When the heads of cauliflower get two to three inches wide, you can tie the tops of the leaves over the developing heads or the sun will turn them a pinkish or purplish color, and they will not be good to eat. The leaves can be tied with twine or even clipped together with big wooden clothespins.

But I think the best way to "blanch" the crop is to tuck a wadded-up piece of aluminum foil inside the leaves. It will keep the light out and allow for better air circulation.

The most common and easily identified lawn weed to herald the return of spring is the bright yellow dandelion. It grows in any soil and will go bananas in full sunlight.

As the yellow flowers mature and ripen, their seed-carrying "puff balls" will travel on the wind for miles, infecting other lawns.

Each mature dandelion has a taproot that grows two to three feet into the soil, so digging them is a real problem. If you break off the taproot in the digging process, it will return to haunt you.

The best control is any 2-4-D product. Do not water or mow for two days after treating your lawn.

People ask me dozens of times every spring which is the best insecticide to use to get the ants off the peonies. The answer is none.

Peony buds have a sugar coating on them, and all the ants are doing is loading up on calories, not harming the plant. In fact, I've read that the sticky coating could prevent the peony buds from opening if the ants weren't there, so leave them alone.

One other thought about peonies: If you look closely at each stem, you will see one large bud at the tip end and smaller buds forming along the stem in the back. Remove the smaller buds. Leave only the large bud. You will have a much better flower display.

I'm often asked why peonies fail to bloom. Often the reason is lack of sun or competition from the roots of nearby shrubs or trees. But the prime reason is because they were planted too deep. The eyes — or buds — of the roots should be no deeper than two inches below the soil. If they get any deeper, you'll never "see" them.

You may notice that some of your evergreen needles are brown or discolored at the tip, or along the margins. The browning is due to desiccation, the loss of moisture from the needles when the ground is frozen and no moisture can be taken from the soil.

April is a good time to fertilize evergreens to help repair the damage. Most evergreens like an "acid-type" fertilizer. The big exception is the taxus, or yew, which does not like acid soil and will be happy with a 10-10-10 fertilizer. That is why you shouldn't plant taxus around acid-loving azaleas or rhododendrons.

You may also notice cracked and split bark on your deciduous trees as a result of the bark freezing at night and thawing in the day. We used to use wound dressings to try to heal these splits, but research indicates that the dressings can do more harm than good. About all you can do is let Mother Nature run her course.

April is a time when you see tent caterpillars crawling into the crotches of cherry and crab-apple trees. Their large white tents can be eliminated with Sevin, Malathion or Spectracide, although a better idea is to use biologically safe Dipel or Thuricide, i.e., bacillus thuringensis, which is totally safe to man.

If you do not want to use any chemicals, prune away the whole branch, drop it in a can and burn it. Either way, only attack the critters close to sundown when they've gone home to the tent after a day of foraging.

FRED'S TIPS

Here's one idea I got from a couple of listeners for getting crops like carrots and beets off to a great start in the spring: Instead of planting them at ground level, plant them in a ridge.

The trick is to take the hoe and work the soil into a ridge about three inches high. Then make a furrow along the ridge about 1/4 inch deep. Plant the seeds in the furrow, covering them with either rotted sawdust or peat moss. Wet the material and keep it damp until the seeds germinate.

I think this method is good because it allows the roots of the carrots and beets to expand in the soil, and the soil cannot become firm or crusty.

Another helpful hint is to place a wide board over the row. Elevate the board an inch or so by supporting it with bricks. That shades the soil, allows it to stay damp, and it's easier for seeds to germinate.

DO NOT apply Sevin during the bloom period of any of your

orchard crops because pesticides are toxic to bees. Bees that aren't killed by direct contact in the orchard often carry the pesticide back to the hive, where it may kill the brood.

Over-mulching can be as dangerous to your crops as running a steamroller through the cabbage patch. It is especially dangerous to shallow-rooted beauties such as azaleas, rhododendrons, dogwoods, boxwoods, hollies and many trees. If you keep adding mulch every year — and some people will pile it up 10 to 12 inches deep — it will suffocate the plant. It will also lead to disease. Two to three inches of mulch is plenty.

People ask me every year what kind of fertilizer to use in the garden. The best answer is to test your soil through your county extension office. It's the only way to determine exactly what you will need to produce healthy vegetables, flowers, shrubs and trees.

But if you did not do that last fall and time is running short, I would recommend that you apply 25 pounds of 5-10-10 or 6-12-12 fertilizer per 1,000 square feet of gardening area. If you plan to grow Sugar Anne snap peas in containers on the patio, add two tablespoons of 5-10-10 or 6-12-12 per bushel of soil.

For better beans, don't plant them in the same space two years in a row. Some diseases will linger in the soil from year to year, causing problems. You can also dust the seeds and the soil bed with a fungicide called Captan.

If you were lucky enough to get a lily for Easter, here's how to take care of it:

Easter lilies need bright, indirect light, not full sun. The soil in the pot should be slightly damp but not soggy. Poke a hole through the decorative foil or remove it completely so the lilies don't get water-soaked toes.

Pick off the yellow tips of the anthers (with tweezers) before they shed their messy pollen. Rotate the pot a quarter turn each day so the lilies will grow straight and not toward the sun.

After the flowers have faded, set the plant outside in full sun. In a week or two, when the plant is acclimated to the outdoors, take it from the pot and put it in a sunny spot in the garden. It may bloom again late the same year, but chances are it will wait and bloom again the following year and last many more years in your garden.

Gardeners often call me in April wondering why their rhubarb develops seed stalks so early in the season. The answer is low fertility in the garden. Rhubarb should be fertilized in early spring with good, all-purpose vegetable garden fertilizer. Be sure to remove the seed stalks that develop this time of year. Don't let the plant go to seed because that will be the end of the crop.

If you lost a landscape tree this past winter and are thinking of replacing it, do not fall for ads about super fast-growing trees. Trees that grow fast usually grow brittle and weak and are often the first to come down in summer windstorms.

If you buy a plant in a container, take a look at the root system as you remove it. If the roots are all matted, take a very sharp knife and cut through them much like you score a ham before putting it in the oven. This will open up the roots and allow them to grow out into the soil instead of in a circle around the rootball.

Here are a few tips for keeping your lovely lilacs, the Perfume Bottles of Spring, healthy and fragrant.

French lilacs, which are now the most popular, should be allowed to grow at least eight feet tall before being thinned out. Cut out a few of the larger stems at ground level to encourage new shoots, and, of course, remove all dead shoots.

The thinning should be done right after they flower, or in winter. A mature French lilac should be 12 to 15 feet tall. Korean lilacs are only 4 to 8 feet tall at maturity.

About the only insect to affect lilacs are stem borers that invade old wood. This is another reason to prune out old, dead wood.

If you want to prune the top to shape the lilac bush, do it right after the spring flowering. Next spring's flowers will develop this summer, and if you wait until fall you'll chop them off. Be sure to fertilize right after the flowering to encourage new buds. Use a balanced fertilizer, like 10-10-10.

It's best to plant or transplant lilacs in the fall, although spring will work with good care and watering. Plant them in full sun in an area that gets good circulation. That will help cut down mildew in the fall. So will sprays of Benlate during the summer.

If an old bush is slowly being taken over by the shadows and roots of a growing tree, dig up the bush, divide the pieces, and get it back in the sun. It may take a few years to bloom again, but it will be worth it.

FRED'S SUPER TIP

If cold, wet spring weather prevented you from getting some of your favorite early spring vegetable seeds sown, don't fret. I've got a suggestion on how you can make up for the lost time: Soak your seeds before you plant them.

Soaking seeds in water prior to planting them is not new.

American Indians filled shallow clay dishes with sand and planted bean seeds in them. The planted dishes were covered with warm ashes for three or four days to speed up germination. As soon as roots began to develop, the beans were dropped into holes in the garden and covered with soil. This procedure was mostly used for planting early crops when the cool soil would tend to rot seeds planted in the usual manner.

Modern-day presoaking is simple. It requires only a small plastic bag, preferably one with a "zipper-lock"-type closing, (shredded) sphagnum moss, or a wet paper towel.

First, let me explain the moss. This is not peat moss. Shredded moss is the long, ropy moss — available at most large garden centers — that is used for lining hanging baskets. This moss contains a natural chemical defense against diseases that can kill seeds as they sprout. Ordinary peat moss should not be used because it does not have this disease-inhibiting agent.

When you open the bag you will find the shredded moss to be as dry as desert sand. You must moisten it before you use it. To do this, roll up a handful of moss in a damp paper towel. Wet the towel again and squeeze the excess moisture out of it.

What you are doing is forcing water into the moss. Repeat the process several times until the moss is thoroughly wet. Then let the towel sit about an hour.

Mark the plastic bag with the seed variety and the date. Tape the front of the seed package to the bag. Put the wet moss in the bag and pour the seeds into the moss. Seal the bag and place it in a warm, light area. Do not use a sunny window. Light is not all that important to germination, and you could cook the seeds if the bag is placed in full sun. I like to put the bag at the foot of our refrigerator. The warm air that circulates there is perfect for this process.

While this is the best way to presprout your seeds, there is a shortcut I have successfully used on occasions. In place of the moss, wet a paper towel and pour the seeds into it. Then put the wet towel in the plastic bag. This will work, but you do not have the natural defense against seed-killing diseases that you have with the shredded moss.

Be ready to plant the sprouted seeds when about half the seeds have pushed out roots or shoots. If rain delays planting, slow down the process by placing the bag in a cooler location.

When planting the sprouted seeds outdoors, do it quickly. Have the soil all worked and the furrow made before you open the bag. Sprouts can be killed by exposure to wind or sunlight.

Don't worry about sprouted seeds being placed upside down or sideways in the furrow. They will straighten themselves out in the sunlight.

NOTES

MAY

MAY CHECKLIST

EARLY
☐ Check holly trees for leaf miner.
☐ Prune evergreens.
☐ Take steps to prevent bacterial wilt of cucumbers
   and melon crops.
☐ Prune rhododendrons.
☐ Move houseplants outdoors.
☐ Repot and fertilize indoor plants.
☐ Buy and plant seedlings for bedding plants.
☐ Plant luffa gourd seeds.

MIDDLE
☐ Check cedar trees for cedar-apple rust gall.
☐ Plant corn in blocks.
☐ Check maple trees for maple petiole borers and wart-like galls.
☐ Check magnolia trees for weevils.
☐ Set out pepper plants when warm enough.
☐ Thin bedding flowers, beets, carrots, loosehead lettuce, onions,
   radishes and spinach.
☐ Check hanging plants for whiteflies and proper moisture.
☐ Remove faded flowers from peonies.

LATE
☐ Pick strawberries.
☐ Divide irises and check for iris borer.
☐ Plant gladioluses.
☐ Thin fruit on apple, pear and peach trees.
☐ Check dogwood trees for borers.
☐ Check roses for "wild growth."
☐ Check evergreens and trees for bagworms.

SUPER TIP
☐ Raising super tomatoes.

May is the month when the flowers are starting to take shape; there's already fresh lettuce, spinach and radishes on the kitchen table, and the awful heat of summer is still on the horizon — right next to the thunderstorms.

May is named for Maia, the Roman goddess of spring and growth, who was probably eight feet tall by her 16th birthday.

The average high temperature for May is 76.2 degrees, the average low is 54.6 degrees, which means you can now get those tomatoes and peppers out into the garden — the pansies.

Average rainfall in May is 4.15 inches. By the end of a "normal" May — if there is such a thing — you should have an accumulation of 19.60 inches of precipitation, about half the average annual total of 43.56 inches.

The rainiest May in history occurred in 1983, when 10.58 inches fell. The driest was 1932, when only .63 inches of rain fell, which is about the era of the Western "Dust Bowl."

The warmest May date in history was May 28, 1911, when the temperature hit 98 degrees. The coldest, speaking of late frosts, was 31 degrees. It happened twice, on May 1, 1963, and May 10, 1966.

The truly awful news is that 1 inch of snow fell in Louisville on May 6, 1898, which was the latest snowfall in history.

There are 13 hours and 47 minutes of sun on May 1, and 14 hours and 37 minutes of sun on May 31. The average soil temperature ranges from 65 to 75 degrees.

May 6, 1856, was the birth date of Sigmund Freud, the founder of psychoanalysis and a man who, if he were alive today, would say we're all nuts to spend so much time in the garden.

EARLY

Often, in the first weeks of May, homeowners complain that the leaves of their holly trees are turning yellow and falling off, and they fear the trees are dying. That is rarely the case. This is the time of year when holly trees normally shed their leaves and develop new ones. Take a close look at your "sick-looking holly," and you should see new leaves developing among the stems.

What you should look for on the fallen leaves are signs of the dreaded leaf miner. If the old leaves have what look like gray tunnels or squiggly lines through them, that's a sure sign they are infected with the leaf miner or leaf maggot.

Look for a tiny black fly darting among the newly unfolding leaves. It's laying the eggs that produce the leaf miner. If you see the fly, apply Malathion. If the black flies haven't found your trees yet but the evidence of leaf miner is there from last year's leaves, then I'd apply a systemic insect control like Cygon or Orthene. Whatever you do, be sure to read the label thoroughly and apply only as directed.

Early to mid-May is often the best time to prune conifers — the cone-bearing evergreens such as pines, spruce and firs. These trees produce their yearly growth in one spurt, the light green bursts at the tips of the limbs that we call "candles." This candling often occurs in early May but could be much earlier during a warm spring.

If you want to shape you tree so it will develop compact, dense growth, prune off the tips of the candles. That will force the tree to develop new shoots below the cut.

Conifers should only be pruned on their candles. If you cut off old growth, it will not regenerate, and your tree can look ugly, if not partially undressed.

It is all right to remove dead or severely damaged limbs close to the trunk, but give that damaged limb a chance to regain its strength before doing anything drastic.

Although your cucumber and muskmelon crops may seem too young and tender to have to worry about "bacterial wilt," now is the time to begin taking measures to prevent it.

Bacterial wilt is the disease that suddenly attacks what appear to be healthy cucumber or melon crops, killing the plants in just a few days. When you cut through the stem of an infected plant, a bead of cloudy, sticky sap can be squeezed from the cut ends. Yuck!

By the time you notice the disease, it's too late to control it. Cucumber beetles, both striped and spotted, have already attacked. They damage the plants by feeding on the leaves, then finish them off with the bacteria they leave behind.

You must begin control early, when seedlings first push up through the ground or the transplants are set. You can use Sevin, diazinon or Rotenone. Spray regularly through the growing season and be sure to spray the undersides of the foliage as well; cucumber beetles can be very sneaky.

Have you pruned those rhododendrons yet? Do it AFTER the flowers have faded. Remove old flowers at their base - just above the point where the new, small green leaves are developing.

If you're pruning to shape the bush, cut as close as possible above a fork or cluster of leaves. Do not leave a long, bare stub. Rhododendrons with long, scraggly stems can be pruned back severely, but the plants may not have many flowers the next season. In following years, the flowers will be more abundant.

In general, however, it's not good to prune back more than one-third of the total number of branches each season. Also, most named varieties of rhododendron are grafted. Cut off any sprouts below the graft because they will not produce the right kind of flowers.

Did you ever fall asleep by the pool, only to wake up feeling as if you'd been scorched to a crisp? Well, houseplants moved outside for the summer — and it's time to think about that — can get a bad case of sunburn too.

Many houseplants, especially those native to the tropics, like the outdoors in the summer. They are used to warm, humid air. We may like air-conditioning in the summer, but when is the last time you saw an air-conditioned nursery or arboretum?

Place your houseplants outdoors in the shade of a nearby tree or tuck them in an outdoor corner where they get all the benefits of humid air and gentle rain but are sheltered from the scorching rays of the sun.

You will have to water more carefully, especially if the plants are in clay pots, because the winds will dry them out more quickly. Also, be sure there is good air circulation around the plants. That will reduce insect and disease problems.

Remember one thing: Your houseplants' outdoor vacation must end when nighttime temperatures fall to about 55 to 60 degrees, which can happen by mid-September.

Every year I get calls from people who ask what they can do to revive houseplants after a cold night outside. Many times the answer is to arrange a decent funeral. Temperatures below 50 degrees can kill many houseplants overnight.

This is a good time of year to repot indoor plants. First, check the bottom of the pots to see if any roots are showing through the drain holes. If they are, you know most of the soil in the pot is full of roots.

For best growth, the plant should be moved to a pot one size larger. Spread some newspapers over a large work area, knock the rootball out of the pot and place it in a larger pot to which you have added drainage material such as small rocks.

Then sift a loose potting soil around the rootball, tamping with your fingers as you fill.

Don't cover the rootball any deeper than it was in its former home. Water well and place in a low-light area for a few days, then return it to its regular place at the window. Wait several weeks before applying plant food. Remember, indoor plants should only be fertilized in the spring and summer, the times they are most active.

What should you do with spring-flowering bulbs after they are finished blooming? You already know to let the foliage die back naturally. Never cut away foliage while it is still green. It's producing food for next year's crop.

If you had problems with animals digging up your bulbs over the winter, put chicken wire over the bulb bed when you plant in the fall. It will prevent anything from digging up your bulbs while allowing enough space for the bulbs to grow.

Every weekend now the nurseries and garden centers will be thick with people buying bedding plants, both flowers and vegetables. Treat these annuals like a carton of ice cream; make them your last purchase before heading home.

Once home, protect the seedlings in a shady spot and water well. They must NEVER dry out. When you finally remove the seedling from its plastic cell pack, don't tug from the top. Push the rootball out by pressing on the bottom and sides of the individual cell.

If the bedding plants are sold in one big tray, take a sharp knife and divide the plants as if you were dividing a pan of brownies. If a knife isn't handy, remove all the seedlings and gently tease individual plants apart with your fingers, trying to keep the rootball intact.

Pop your plants into the garden as quickly as possible. If you must plant on a sunny day, wait until late afternoon and mist and water the plants thoroughly as you plant. A very diluted solution of water-soluble fertilizer will help.

It helps to shade the seedlings for three to five days with strawberry baskets, cardboard or a board elevated on bricks. One inventive gardener I know collects old umbrellas and uses them as sunshades. It looks strange, but it works.

For a little gardening fun, consider planting seeds for luffa gourds, which can be used as sponges after they mature.

MIDDLE

If you see an orangish, jellylike mass growing on the branches of your cedar tree, chances are it's cedar-apple rust gall. The galls, ranging from one to two inches in diameter, will keep growing until they fall off the tree. If you have apple trees nearby, remove the galls by hand and destroy them. Do not plant apple trees anywhere near cedar trees because spores from the gall are carried by the wind to the apple trees, infecting the leaves and fruits.

Your baby sprouts of sweet corn will never develop into succulent ears of corn unless you plant the corn in blocks, not one or two long rows.

That's because the corn silks that grow out of the top of the ear — each is attached to one individual kernel on the cob — most be pollinated by the pollen produced by the tassels at the top of the cornstalk. If you plant the corn in one or two straight rows, the wind is liable to blow the pollen the other direction, resulting in poor pollination.

So if you're planting as few as 12 stalks of corn, plant them in three rows with four stalks per row. The same concept holds true if you are planting 120 stalks.

Corn likes a high-nitrogen fertilizer when it is planted and again when it is knee-high. As the ears develop, the corn earworm can be a pest, but it is easily controlled with Sevin.

May is not a time of year normally associated with falling maple leaves, but it can be when the maple petiole borer is at work. The borer has a definite life cycle. The adult female sawfly emerges in May and lays eggs on the stems of the leaves. When the eggs hatch, yellow, wormlike larvae emerge and begin tunneling into the leaf stalk. As the worm matures, it eats most of the inside of the stem and — pfffft! — the leaf is blown off the tree by the wind.

The worms remain inside the stem. Later on, when the stem falls to the earth, the worms bore into the ground, lay eggs for the sawfly, and the cycle is complete.

What can you do about it? Nothing. The tree damage is minimal. There are still plenty of leaves left for the autumn drop.

Maple leaves are also susceptible to small, wartlike galls that come in a variety of shapes and colors, including red, green and black.

The cause is a mite that spends the winter in the bark of the tree, then moves to the leaves in the spring to feed. As the mites feed on the underside of the leaves, the leaves produce pouchlike galls enclosing the mites. As with the maple petiole borer, they do not cause enough damage to worry about, especially if the tree is fertilized on scheduled.

The large, glossy, evergreen leaves of Southern magnolias are also susceptible to insect problems in the spring. Around here the culprit is generally the night-feeding sassafras weevil, also called the yellow poplar weevil or the magnolia leaf miner.

The adult weevil survives the winter in the leaf litter below the tree. Then, in its beetle stage, it flies to the trees to feed on buds and developing leaves. It will produce big holes in the leaves as well as brown blotches near the leaf tip.

Sevin is the best control. In spraying the tree I would add a drop or two of liquid soap, which helps the spray stick to the glossy surface. Or you can buy what is called "spreader sticker" at garden centers, a special substance that holds the pesticide to the leaves.

Sweet or pungent, long or blocky, hot or mild, the pepper is often the pickiest plant in the spring vegetable patch. That's because peppers do not like cool weather. Do not set them out until night temperatures have risen well above 55 degrees, which can be well into the month of May. Planting peppers too early often results in stunted plants and poor yields.

You can get peppers off on the road to success with a high-phosphorous starter fertilizer such as 8-24-8. Do not give them any additional fertilizer until a good fruit set has developed. You must harvest the fruit regularly so new fruit will set and always rotate tomatoes, eggplant and pepper crops, making sure they do not follow each other in the same location. They are all susceptible to the same soil-borne diseases.

You may feel like Jack the Ripper, but when it comes to gardens, thinning plants is very important to their growth. It's not an easy thing to do. You have just spent weeks worrying about every one on them, and now you're being asked to rip many of them out.

It must be done. With many

plants — and carrots and turnips come quickly to mind — the biggest reason they "go to tops" is because they were not thinned out properly when they were little. They didn't have sufficient space to grow healthy bottoms. In cases such as large-flowering zinnias and marigolds, it helps prevent them from growing into weak-kneed skyscrapers that are easily toppled in summer rainstorms.

You should consider all bedding flowers, as well as beets, carrots, loose-leaf lettuce, onions, radishes and spinach, as candidates for thinning. Pick a time when the ground is damp and soft but not muddy. If the ground has been dry, you should water for an hour beforehand.

Look at the seed package to find the recommended spacing for each variety or check the accompanying vegetable-planting guide. As a rule you can start thinning when your plants have one or two pairs of true leaves — not counting the "seed leaves," which emerge first. Onions should be thinned when they are three to four inches tall.

Gently pull out the unwanted plants without disturbing those that remain. If the remaining plants are disturbed, firm the soil around them, or if the stand is very thick, cut the tops off with scissors, leaving the roots of the neighboring plants undisturbed.

Evening is the best time to thin because the plants will have the cool night to recover.

You can thin vegetables in several stages until the remaining plants are the right distance apart, using the thinnings for taste treats. Many of the flowers you thin, and a few of the vegetables, may be transplanted to other parts of the garden or shared with neighbors. But root crops such as beets, carrots and radishes may develop malformed roots and do not transplant well.

Mid-May is a time when most people find it difficult to resist buying hanging baskets, giving little thought to how much care they will need in the hotter months of June and July.

Fuchsia, for example, are big sellers in the spring but are often dead by July because they can't handle direct sun; they need only a little bit of filtered light in the morning.

Don't ever let the soil of a hanging plant go completely dry. Mist daily and watch for whiteflies, which dearly love fuchsia. Hanging baskets need pots 10 to 12 inches in diameter, preferably ones made of plastic because they will hold water longer. Use a peatlike potting mix for the best growth and be sure the plants have excellent drainage.

If the leaves of a few of your vegetables, especially potatoes or radishes, are beginning to look as if they were shot full of holes, the likely culprit is the flea beetle. The flea beetle is a very tiny black, brown or metallic-blue bug that often emerges in May.

Its enlarged hind legs enable it to jump like a flea when disturbed. Control is very important because the flea beetles' tiny white larvae feed on roots and seldom can be seen underground. The adults, of course, feed above ground, filling the leaves with tiny holes. Fortunately, Sevin and diazinon will control them.

Be sure to remove the faded flowers from your peonies now. If you let the old blossoms go to seed, they will sap the strength from next year's crop. But don't move peonies now unless it's an emergency. The best time to re-plant, divide or establish new varieties is in late September or October.

LATE

You should be out picking strawberries, if you haven't already been out in the patch sneaking a few of the early ones. And like everything else in life, there is a right way and a wrong way to harvest berries.

Plan A, of course, is to grasp the stem between the forefinger and thumbnail just above the berry. Pull with a slight twisting motion. When the stem breaks, let the berry roll into the palm of your hand. When you have three or four berries in your hand, carefully place the berries in a container. Don't overfill — strawberries stacked over five inches deep will mash the fruit on the bottom.

That's Plan A. University of Kentucky extension specialist Jerry Brown suggests another way to harvest berries: Eat them immediately after picking, and you'll never have to worry about bruises.

After the irises have finished blooming, usually in late May or early June, is the best time to dig and divide them. When you dig a clump you will find many new plants off the sides of the original rhizome. Carefully remove the new plants. But before discarding the old ones, check to see if the roots are riddled with holes, sometimes to the point where they're almost hollow. If they are, the iris borer has paid a visit.

The moth of the adult borer flies at night, laying eggs in fall that will hatch into larvae in the spring. The larvae can be killed with weekly applications of Sevin or Malathion, if they are used from the time growth begins until the end of May. Older larvae can be killed with a systemic insecticide like Cygon. The borer is the iris's biggest enemy, mostly because it introduces a bacteria that causes a soft rot.

Remember when replanting healthy irises to leave the very top of their root sticking out of the soil, much like ducks in water. Don't trim off the leaves; they provide nourishment.

May is a good time to plant gladioluses. With a little planning, you can have these versatile flowers blooming all summer and fall.

Glads, which produce large, showy blossoms along a long, pointed stalk, get their name from "gladius," the Latin word for sword. There is no other cut flower that offers the reds, pinks, yellows, whites, purples and lavenders it produces.

Glads are grown from corms, sensitive, bulblike structures that must be dug up every fall and replanted every spring. Depending on the cultivar, glads take from 60 to 120 days to produce flowers that will bloom for two weeks. Some of the taller varieties need staking to keep from falling over under the weight of their own blooms.

Glad bulbs will open at the bottom of the spike. Cut the flowers after at least three florets have opened. As the lower florets fade, the rest will open. Allow as many leaves as possible to remain on the plant so it will store food for next year.

Now is a good time to thin out the developing fruit on apple, peach and pear trees. This will not only increase the yield but will also eliminate alternate-year bearing, which is the problem when a fruit tree bears heavily one year and has little or no fruit the next.

Some home fruit growers inadvertently thin their trees every spring by using Sevin, which kills the bees needed for pollination. Do not apply Sevin from the time the trees bloom to five weeks after bloom.

Peaches should be thinned four to six weeks after bloom. There should be four to six inches between each fruit. Apples and pears should be thinned between 30 and 60 days after bloom. There should be six to eight inches between each fruit.

Late May, around Memorial Day weekend, is the time to spray Lindane on your beloved dogwood trees to kill the dreaded dogwood borer, an insect that often damages our favorite spring tree by eating holes into it.

Check your tree regularly for the damage — holes and sawdust. Dogwoods grown out in full sun — they prefer to be understory trees — seem more vulnerable to the borer. It can be controlled with sprays of Lindane along the trunk and lower limbs, which insures that the insecticide will be on the bark when the young borers hatch and begin entering the tree. Also, be sure to avoid attacking the shins of the dogwood with your lawn mower. Those gashes provide openings for disease. You can also spray for dogwood borers in August as a follow-strike, but May is best.

Check your roses to see if they are "going wild" — blooming from beneath the bud union or from their roots. That's not the growth you want on a hybrid plant.

This wild growth can occur when a bud union freezes or dies, or if the plant roots dry out. Wild growth will have smaller, light-colored leaves and should be cut away. Chances are the wild growth will produce an inferior plant; if you had a guarantee with your purchase, you should exercise it.

Late May is also the time when bagworm larvae begin to hatch and crawl out of their tiny bags in search of food. The larvae, the most common pests to evergreens in this area, can strip shrubs of all their foliage, even killing them. They will also attack maple trees, roses and flowering quince.

The bags are very small — you may have to search carefully to find them. If there are only a few on the tree, they can be removed by hand. If the infestation is heavy, they should be sprayed with Malathion, Orthene, diazinon or Dylox, or the biological control, Dipel or Thuricide.

FRED'S TIPS

If you have a serious love for cucumbers and little room to grow them, you can nearly double your harvest by growing them in a wire cage or up a trellis. A study at Louisiana State University indicated that fruit set almost doubled when the plants were allowed to grow up instead of out. The plants grew bigger leaves and had better access to the sun, and the amount of fruit rot was reduced.

You must help the plant tendrils get started on the wire. One week after they've begun to bloom, side-dress them with 1/2 cup of 10-10-10 fertilizer. Repeat in three weeks. Don't worry. The vines will be strong enough to support even big cucumbers.

What type of flowers will do best in a hot, dry area or adapt especially well to a long drought? Around here, your best flowering bets are zinnias, ornamental peppers, cosmos, vinca, portulaca or moss rose, verbena, celosia or cockscomb, ageratum, cleome, gazania and gerbera. For the vegetable garden try okra, lima beans, amaranth, small cherry tomatoes and hot peppers. I had especially good luck with an ornamental pepper called "candlelight," an edible hot pepper.

Newspapers topped with grass clippings make an especially nice mulch because there is nothing to pick up after the gardening season is over; just let it decompose and plow it under. Even with the terrible summer of 1988 I only had to water my cherry tomatoes four times because we'd mulched so well. Don't use paper with colored ink, however.

Black plastic will work in some areas but should not be used around permanent plantings like foundation evergreens. It will not decompose. It can suffocate root systems and makes the plants difficult to water.

When you do water, water deeply. Merely sprinkling the garden encourages shallow root growth, which is detrimental to your plants. Try to water early in the day. Sometimes you can't avoid watering late in the day — Mother Nature, in fact, has been known to loosen her rain clouds at night — but wet foliage is conducive to the development of night-stalking diseases.

In long periods of drought, soak your trees and shrubs thoroughly with a hose.

If your lawn is heavily shaded by large trees, especially maples, you will probably never get a strong stand of grass. My advice is to plant ground covers.

One of most attractive ground covers in our area is ajuga, or carpet bugleweed. Its glossy green foliage turns a bronzy green in the fall, and the plant has a show of bright blue flower spikes in late summer.

If you have a steep slope, liriope, also called lilyturf and monkey grass, has spiky blades eight to 12 inches tall. In July and

August it sends up tall spikes of lavender or white flowers. It's tough, easily adaptable, winter hardy and divides easily if you want to start it somewhere else. There are whole sections of seed catalogs dedicated to ground covers, so check them out.

Cinder blocks will not only provide a retaining wall for your herb beds, but you can also plant herbs in the holes in the blocks, giving you a little more space to grow. Since most commonly grown herbs need a slightly alkaline soil — pH 7 to 8 — the blocks will constantly leach lime into the soil, helping to maintain the pH level. However, you will need a blend of topsoil, sand, sphagnum moss and a little agricultural lime as a soil mix for the blocks. You'll also have to water often because small patches of soil tend to dry out more quickly.

If you buy a flower or vegetable transplant in a peat pot, never, never let any part of the pot stick above the soil level when you put it in the ground. If you do, the peat pot will act as a wick, drawing moisture from the plant's soil and allowing it to evaporate into the air.

If you can't remove the peat pot because the plant's root system has grown into it, tear away the top lip of the pot so it will not be in contact with the air. I once saw a whole garden of peppers and tomatoes die because peat pots were not buried deep enough.

Every year I get calls from people who applied the wrong kind of chemicals to their garden and then wonder if they can still harvest their vegetables. The answer is always NO! They must start over again.

I cannot stress enough that you must read the labels on all chemicals and apply accordingly. If the label says a plant should not be picked for a certain time after spraying, don't pick it. If the label says one tablespoon is good, don't ever think two tablespoons is better. It's not. If you only follow one piece of advice, follow that. Your health is at stake.

Many people will see an infestation of winged ants near their houses — especially during a warm spring — and fear the worst: termites.

The best way to tell the winged ant from the termite is to examine the wings. Termites have two pairs of wings of equal length. Flying ants also have two pairs of wings, but they are unequal in length. Also, the termite has a thick waist; the waist of a flying ant is pinched in.

If it still looks likes termites, don't panic. Termites work slowly. Call two or three pest-control companies for examinations and estimates. Be sure the firm is licensed and that its employees have ID cards issued by the state division of pesticides. Also, be sure to ask for references.

Old-fashioned manure is a good fertilizer that supplies mostly nitrogen to the soil. But spring is not the best time to apply manure because it often gives off ammonia that can "burn" plants and can even irritate the human who applies it. A good friend once had the hair on his arms singed by fresh ammonia. The best time to apply manure to the garden is the fall so it has time to cool down before going to work on plants, and letting it age under plastic will help, and improve the view..

If you bought ladybugs to release in your garden to control the bad bugs, you could be disappointed. The ladybugs may have "itchy wings."

According to the U. S. Department of Agriculture, mail-order ladybugs are collected from their hibernating quarters in California canyons.

These ladybugs don't come with a sense of duty or a road map. They will usually disappear, leaving your garden miles behind while searching for cultivated fields. The ladybugs you find in your garden are the local variety. The people your mail-order ladybugs visit after you release them will be grateful, but they won't know whom to thank.

Crab-apple trees in our area are susceptible to apple-scab disease if extended wet periods occur as the trees are developing leaves. Severely infected trees will show yellow leaves and suffer premature leaf drop. They

can be sprayed with fungicides following wet periods, but the best and cheapest answer is to purchase only trees that are disease-resistant. Crab apples are lovely ornamentals, but only if you buy the right kind.

One handy way to remove the old blossoms from your azalea plant is with a broom. But be gentle, or you will damage the plant. It's also a good time to apply a high-acid fertilizer around the plants. Repeat in June. Keep them watered. Azaleas have shallow roots.

FRED'S SUPER TIP

It doesn't matter how good a gardener you think you are, the one vegetable we measure most gardeners by is the tomato.

The traditional time to plant tomatoes is after Derby Day. You can plant earlier, but chances are you'll be out there covering the plants on many frosty evenings.

If you buy tomato plants, choose short, stocky, healthy-looking ones, and buy a package of water-soluble tomato food like 5-10-5 while you're at it. A lot of people make the mistake of buying the biggest plant in the gardening center, the one that looks as if it might blossom first. It might, but in the long run a smaller, nicely shaped plant will bear more fruit.

Whether buying your seedlings or beginning them at home, choose varieties that say V.F.N. or V.F.N.T. That's not some sort of secret code to keep the Russians off-guard. It indicates the variety's resistance to verticillium wilt, fusarium wilt, tobacco mosaic and nematodes (those small insects that attack root systems).

Also, consider the variety. A determinate tomato is one that will be bushy and not grow more than five feet tall. An indeterminate plant will grow taller and bloom all summer, producing new fruits until frost.

Check the number of days from first blooming to picking. Early Girl plants, for instance, will produce tomatoes in 54 days. Better Boy, one of the most popular varieties around here, will take about 70 days. Because there are dozens of varieties, you can have tomatoes from late June until frost if you plan carefully.

Another mistake home gardeners often make with tomatoes is not planting them deep enough. Any part of the stem without leaves should be planted underground. One year I found a tomato plant with 12 inches of bare stem, and I buried it horizontally, bending the top upward so only its tip was above ground. New roots developed all along the stem, and it did very well.

For years now I've been growing my tomatoes in cages, and they love it. It eliminates the chore of tying the plants to the stake. They show less crack and sunburn, ripen more uniformly and produce fewer culls.

You can use concrete reinforcing wire for cages, but it will need painting. Old "hog wire" will make nice cages. The wire should be about 76 inches long, which will curl into a nice-sized cage, and 60 inches high. Anchor it with a stake.

The most important part of the whole tomato-growing season is using mulch. It's the best way to prevent blossom-end rot, that dark, leathery scar you will often see on the bottom of the tomato in hot weather. It's a disease blamed on a calcium deficiency in the soil because of constant fluctuations in soil moisture. Mulching helps prevent that.

Finally, you can't do much bragging about your tomatoes unless you can take one over to the neighbor's house. I had a call a few years ago from someone who followed my suggestion of caging tomatoes, only he had the hardest time getting them out of the cage. He'd used chicken wire.

NOTES

JUNE

JUNE CHECKLIST

EARLY

☐ Spray dogwoods to prevent borer infestation.
☐ Divide and reset irises.
☐ Set out caladiums, cannas and elephant ears.
☐ Renovate strawberry patch.
☐ Mulch garden.
☐ Plant Halloween pumpkins.
☐ Spray tomatoes with fruit-setting hormone.
☐ Prune privet hedge.
☐ Continue thinning fruit on trees.
☐ Inspect trees and evergreens for bagworms.
☐ Trim tops off peony bushes.
☐ Water garden and newly planted trees.

MIDDLE

☐ Prune climbing roses and apply fungicide.
☐ Stop harvesting asparagus and rhubarb.
☐ Start seeds (cabbage, broccoli and brussels sprouts)
   for fall garden.
☐ Rip out any spinach, radishes and lettuce that has "bolted" and
   plant beans or corn in its place.
☐ Pinch back mums, coleus and impatiens.
☐ Check cucumbers, melons and squash for cucumber beetles.
☐ Check tomatoes for early blight.
☐ Check a few potato plants for blackleg.
☐ Pinch faded blooms and seed pods off petunias, water and
   fertilize.

LATE

☐ Spray grass for sod webworms.
☐ Check pepper plants for bacterial leaf spot.
☐ Check houseplants and water often.
☐ Continue spraying fruit trees.
☐ Pick raspberries before they become overripe to avoid sap beetles.
☐ Check to be sure that potatoes, carrots and onions are covered
   with dirt.
☐ Remove foliage and transplant bulbs from spring-flowering plants.
☐ Remove suckers from tomato plants.
☐ Sow quick-growing annuals.

SUPER TIP

☐ Raising super roses.

June is the month when you can't see the trees for all the canning jars, kettles and preservatives stacked up on the kitchen table. All that time in the garden is paying off — with more time in the kitchen.

It's a month that was named for Juno, the Roman's patron goddess of marriage, although a second theory says June is taken from the Latin word **juniores,** or "young men," who were especially honored by the Romans in that month. Actually, both men and women get together for weddings in June — many of them outdoors.

The average high temperature in the Louisville area in June is 84 degrees; the average low 63.3 degrees. The average rainfall is 3.60 inches, a drop from March, April and May.

The wettest June in Louisville history was the 10.11 inches that fell in 1960; the driest was the .35 inches in 1936. In Kentucky lore, however, that palls to the 10.40 that fell on little Dunmor in one 24-hour period on June 28, 1960.

Scottsville, Ky., won a spot of dubious distinction on June 23, 1969, when 8.85 inches of rain fell on the city in just six hours. That's a lot, but on June 26, 1943, Berea College in Eastern Kentucky recorded 3.87 inches of rain in one hour.

The warmest June day on record was June 28, 1944, when the thermometer hit 103. The coldest was June 1, 1966, when the temperature hit 42 degrees and 300,000 tomatoes left for Florida.

There are 14 hours and 38 minutes of sun on June 1, and 14 hours and 47 minutes on June

30. The longest day of the year is June 21 when the sun is up 14 hours and 49 minutes. The average soil temperature in June ranges from 75 to 83 degrees.

Kentucky became the 15th state to join the union on June 1, 1792. Jeff Davis, president of the Confederacy, was born in Kentucky on June 3, 1808.

EARLY

Unless you did it around Memorial Day, you'd better hurry to protect your precious dogwood trees from the dogwood borer with sprays of Lindane.

The borer is a major problem for dogwoods, and it is a particular pest if the dogwoods are in

full sun. A University of Kentucky study showed that the probability of dogwood-borer infestation was 68 percent in full sun, 50 percent in partial shade and 21 percent in full shade.

Wounding, generally caused by lawn mowers, also increased the likelihood of infestation; up to 78 percent for severe wounding and 40 percent for slight wounding.

So it's best to plant dogwoods in the shade, mulch around the tree to avoid lawn-mower damage and use Lindane on the Memorial Day weekend, or soon afterward. Be sure to heavily wet the trunk from the soil line up to the bottom limbs.

A reminder that overcrowded clumps of bearded iris can be divided and reset during June.

Dig the clumps and wash them off with a hose to reveal rot or borer damage. Cut away any infected parts with a sharp knife and divide the healthy portions into single or paired rhizomes.

To prevent infection, dust the rhizomes with Captan before replanting. Cut the foliage in half, or shorter, and reset the rhizomes no more than one inch deep. Be sure the very top of the rhizome is at ground level. If it's too deep, the flower will not bloom properly.

Be sure to break the seed pods off the plants you don't move so their energy can be devoted to new growth.

The soil temperature should be warm enough to get those caladiums, cannas and elephant-ear plants into the ground. Don't plant them too soon; they don't like anything below 70 degrees and will refuse to grow if it's cooler. They need lots of water once they're in the ground.

Now that strawberry picking is over, it's time to wash the red stains off your fingers and renovate the patch for next year. With new plantings, the crop usually drops off after the second season, but you can help keep it vital by mowing the leaves to a height of two to three inches. As hard as it might be to do, you should also cultivate the space between the rows and thin the plants to about 18 inches apart. Then apply a general-purpose fertilizer between the rows at a rate of five pounds per 100 feet.

Finally, the runners should be encouraged to root and form new plants.

A reminder that if you want to have ready access to your garden later this summer while your neighbor is wading around knee-high in weeds trying to find his zucchini, it's time to put down mulch.

For as long as I've been doing the "Weekend Gardener," I've advocated using newspapers and grass clippings. Wet the papers first to make them easier to handle, then place them eight to 10 pages thick. Work soil around the edges of the paper with a hoe, then spread the grass clippings two to three inches thick. Don't use too much grass because it gets very hot as it decomposes. Keep adding clippings as the grass rots. At the end of the season, plow it all under.

As odd as it sounds, June is the perfect time to plant the perfect Halloween pumpkin. That's because many of the best pumpkins take about 90 days to mature. If they're planted in May, they will mature in August and may go soft by the time Halloween rolls around.

So check the growing days on the back of the seed package and plant accordingly. If pumpkins must be picked before Halloween because of a heavy frost, store them in a cool, dry place.

This is the time of year when home gardeners notice that the first blossoms are falling off their tomato plants, a crisis nearly as bad as the children growing up and leaving home.

This often happens when there are night temperatures below 60 degrees or on extremely hot days, neither of which are conducive to setting fruit.

Spraying the clusters with a fruit-setting hormone such as Blossom Set helps alleviate the problem and could give you tomatoes three weeks sooner than your neighbor, which is well-worth the price.

Early spring is always the best time to plant or prune your privet hedges. If your 10-year-old privet hedge is looking scraggly and hopeless, it can be cut within six inches of the ground and retrained into a decent hedge. Privets can be cut just about anytime the shears are sharp. Be sure to prune it in "triangular fashion," thicker at the bottom than at the top.

If you notice your fruit trees are shedding small fruits this time of year, don't worry about it; the drop is just nature's way of taking care of overpopulation.

Most trees have at least two waves of fruit drop, the first right after blooming and the second three to four weeks later, often in June. Since only one bloom in 20 is needed for a good crop, the natural drop won't do much harm.

In fact, chances are you'll have to help nature along in June by thinning the apple crop to about one fruit every six to eight inches. Peaches and plums should be thinned to one fruit every four to five inches.

Early June is also the time to inspect your juniper, arborvitae

and other trees for bagworms. They'll soon be hanging from the limbs in spindly shaped bags about two inches long. The bags contain worms that feed on a wide variety of deciduous trees and evergreens.

Pick off the bags you can reach and burn them or throw them in the garbage. If it appears that the worms have already hatched, spray with Sevin, Malathion or bacillus thuringensis, which is also called Dipel or Thuricide.

Be sure to snip those ugly tops off your peony bushes to get them on the road to beauty for next year. If your peony has been in the ground several years and still hasn't bloomed, chances are you planted it too deep. Mark it with a stick and make a note to replant it in the fall. A happy, blooming peony bush can go decades without being transplanted.

This is a critical time for watering the garden. Those long June dry spells can weaken plants so badly they might not recover. Your garden needs at least an inch or two of water every week. Occasional light sprinkling of the garden or the lawn does more harm than good.

Put a rain gauge next to your garden and if it's coming up short, break out the sprinkler.

Also, don't neglect newly planted trees, even the ones you planted last year. Death by drought can occur even two or three years later. Let the hose run over them for 20 minutes.

MIDDLE

Be sure to prune your climbing roses right after the blossoms fade and apply a fungicide to prevent and control black spot. If you cut some of your other flowers to take indoors, be sure you cut them again just before placing them in water and add a floral preservative to keep them fresh. Changing water frequently helps too.

You should have stopped harvesting rhubarb and asparagus by now to allow the plants to develop and store food for next year's asparagus salad or rhubarb pie. Fertilize and water to keep them going.

If you're thinking about a fall garden of cabbage, broccoli and brussels sprouts, now is the time to start your seeds. Use the same methods you used in the spring, only keeping the soil warm shouldn't be as much of a problem. Remember, it's only about 190 shopping days until Christmas.

Once we hit mid-June, all that lovely spinach and lettuce and those rows of radishes are going to "bolt" in the hot weather, turn ugly and go to seed. You might as well rip them out, refer-

tilize and consider second plantings of beans or corn in the same place.

One sure way to get bushier growth from your mums, coleus and impatiens is to pinch back the shoot tips. It's especially important to pinch back the mums now, or they will be too leggy this fall.

Mid-June is the time you may notice that some of your cucumber, melon and squash plants are dying for no apparent reason. The culprit is often the cucumber beetle, a black-and-yellow-striped vermin that carries a disease called bacterial wilt. There is no known cure, so spray your plants regularly with Sevin to control the pests.

If the weather has been warm and very moist, check your tomatoes for early blight, a disease that first appears as circular to angular brown or black spots on the lower leaves. Pinch off the leaf and apply a fungicide like Maneb.

The same kind of weather will produce blackleg on potato plants, an awful disease in which the stems turn black from the ground level up into the plant. As it spreads, the plants turn yellow and die. There's no cure for blackleg. Check the plants at random and dig up the diseased ones, use certified seed potatoes next time and don't plant potatoes in that spot for at least a year.

The petunia is one of those flowers that looks so nice when you bring it home but a month later is about as appealing as a dead dust mop. The secret to petunias is regular care. Keep the faded blooms pinched off, but don't just pull off the flower. You must also pinch away that tiny seed pod at the base of the flower or that stem will die back as the seeds ripen.

Be sure to water often and fertilize lightly every third week with a high-phosphorous fertilizer like 5-10-5 or 5-10-10. Plants that become too leggy by midsummer can be cut way back, and they will bloom until fall.

LATE

Late June is one of the two times to spray your grass for the sod webworm, the insect that often causes brown, unsightly patches in your lawn. When mowing you may see an increase in the number of small, gray moths that get up in front of the mower and "skitter" over the top of the ground. That's the female moths dropping their sod webworm eggs onto the soil. It's also time to spray with diazinon, and be sure to water it into the soil. Mid-August is the second time to spray.

Hot, rainy June weather can also produce bacterial leaf spot in peppers. The disease looks like brown or tan spots on leaves, which then turn yellow and fall, often leaving a carpet of leaves below the plant. It can be controlled with sprays of fixed copper every seven to 10 days.

Be sure to keep a close eye on the houseplants that have been set outdoors. They should be growing vigorously, will need more water than they did indoors and don't want direct, scalding sun.

Be sure to continue your fruit-spraying schedule. As the fruit develops, you may have to prop up some of the limbs to keep them from breaking off. It takes a lot of work to keep a good home orchard going.

If you notice tiny black bugs on your raspberries, they're probably sap beetles, which literally make a living from overripe fruit. The obvious solution is to get those berries off the bush and into your mouth, or freezer, as quickly as possible.

Check your potato plants, the sensitive shoulders of your carrots and even your onion bulbs to be sure they are covered with dirt. If you don't, the potato tubers will turn green and become inedible, and the carrots and onions will taste bad. Also keep a constant check for potato beetles. Thiodan is the best bet to kill them.

By now it's safe to remove all the yellow foliage from the spring-flowering bulbs, if you haven't already done it. The bulbs can also be transplanted now, but be sure to add some bone meal or fertilizer. If you wait to transplant, you'll probably forget where they are.

Although not vital to the health of the plant, removing suckers from tomatoes will help preserve their energy and produce more fruit. Suckers, the big shoots that develop sideways from the main stem, can be picked off and rooted in sand or peat moss to get you going on a fall garden. I know one gardener who buys three tomato plants in the spring and winds up with a dozen or more just by rooting the suckers.

June is a great month to sow some quick-growing annuals like marigolds, ageratum or zinnias from seed. That way you'll have fresh flowers just about the time the other annuals are pooping out. Just be sure to mark the spot so they don't get lost in the jungle.

FRED'S TIPS

Be careful that the herbicides you use to treat your lawn don't drift onto your garden crops. (Be aware of this even if you hire someone to treat your lawn.) These weedkillers can distort the growth of cucumbers and even knock the baby buds off the vine. Tomatoes and snap beans are also sensitive to weedkillers. So don't apply herbicides on windy or rainy days if you are anywhere near the garden.

Here's a reminder that spraying with insecticides — especial-

ly Sevin — should be done in late afternoon or evening when the bees have gone home for the day. The bees are vital to the transfer of pollen that produces the fruit, and they are very susceptible to Sevin.

Horticulture advisers at the University of Kentucky have begun to notice that many newly planted trees and shrubs do not grow properly because their roots have been balled in synthetic burlap.

Natural burlap will decompose quickly, allowing the roots to spread. But the synthetic, plastic-like material may last for years, inhibiting root growth. So check the wrapping around your dismal-looking plant, and if it feels and looks like plastic, you will have to dig up the plant, remove the synthetic material and replant the tree. Be sure to wait until fall, however, before doing this.

You'll see a lot of nurseries and discount stores offering sales on trees this time of year, but this late in the season is a very risky time to plant, and most places will not give guarantees with their sales. You're better off waiting until fall.

If you want to take a chance, buy some potted plants and shrubs at discount prices, nurse them through at home until planting time in the fall. Keep them very well watered, and in partial sun. You might even heel them into a trench in the ground, still in the container.

You can save a lot of money buying bargains, but you may need it for funerals.

One strong word about the "topping" of large trees such as maples: DON'T.

That kind of topping, which many homeowners believe will save time picking up fallen limbs, severely weakens a tree, and the tree could be blown down in the next storm. Topping a tree only stimulates dozens of new shoots, none of which are as strong as the originals. Just don't do it.

One common belief among gardeners is that squash should not be planted next to cucumbers, muskmelons or watermelons because they will cross-pollinate, producing a strange-tasting fruit. That is not true. Any cross-pollination will affect the seeds produced by the fruit and not the taste. If you save those seeds, however, and planted them the following year, you might come up with a muskcumber.

This is the time of year when gardeners often complain that their squash is putting out lots of flowers but no fruit. The reason is that baby squash plants often produce mostly male flowers — with the female flowers to follow.

If you don't know the difference, look below the flower; the female flower will have a swollen ovary or a tiny squash. The male does not.

Here's something to keep you going while you're waiting. Pick some male blossoms. Mix one tablespoon of water with one egg and beat well. Add salt and pepper to flour or cornmeal. Place cooking oil in deep-fryer or use 1/4 cup of cooking oil in an iron skillet.

When the oil is hot, dip the blossoms into the egg mixture, roll them in the flour and fry them separately until brown. The taste is similar to mushrooms.

Don't overfertilize peppers and other "leafy" vegetables with nitrogen or you'll end up with beautiful foliage and no fruit. You must also harvest peppers regularly, or they will stop producing.

If you have a mouse-chasing cat around your house, here's a way that feline can help with gardening: Save your empty cat-food cans and use them as a defense against cutworms, those small, noxious grubs that will chop off your plants at the ground line.

The greasy-brown to gray grubs work at night after spending the day curled up in the soil. But if you cut the tops and bottoms out of the cans and cut the sides of the cans and then put them around your broccoli or cabbage plants like collars, the plants will be safer. Be sure the cans are buried about an inch deep.

If some of those spring thunderstorms are knocking down your peony bushes — and doesn't it seem as if there's always a bad storm the week they hit full bloom — try putting little fences around them in the same manner you cage tomatoes, only not as high. It works wonders.

Speaking of thunderstorms, the U.S. Department of Agriculture advises that a freezer fully loaded with crops from your garden will stay cold for one or two days in the event of a power failure. Even if the meat and poultry have thawed, the USDA says you can refreeze them provided the meat and poultry still have ice crystals or have stayed below 40 degrees for less than two days. Just don't open the door every 45 seconds to check.

Ticks are a summer problem no one really likes to talk about, so let's get this over quickly. To remove a tick from the skin, grasp it as close to the skin as possible and pull upward, using steady, even pressure. Don't jerk it or twist it.

Now here's the really bad news: Keep the tick in a jar. Ticks can cause disease, and if the person bitten by the tick gets sick in a few weeks, the captured tick may help doctors identify the problem.

All right, we've talked about ticks, so let's do chiggers and get it over with. Chiggers, as every gardener knows, are what cause those red, itchy spots about an hour after you're back in the house. They are actually little insects about 1/15 of an inch long that live in tall grass. Their instincts are to rush to bite people where clothing fits the tightest, such as waistbands, or worse.

Chiggers don't burrow into the skin. They bite, feed, remain on the skin surface and fall off, only you don't know they were there until they are gone.

Use insect repellent before going out and take a hot, soapy shower when you come back inside. Several skin ointments can also reduce the itching.

A guaranteed way to increase your houseplant population comes from the Purdue University department of agriculture.

June, it says, is a great time to propagate indoor plants. As the days grow longer and brighter, houseplants put on a good flush of growth, and the actively growing tips make the best material for cutting.

The best plants to use are the easily rooted varieties such as coleus, wandering Jew, philodendron, ivy and peperomia, but don't hesitate to experiment with others.

Or if you want to be more adventurous, you can propagate the dieffenbachia (dumb cane) by cutting the stem into many sections, as long as each stem has one bud. And plants like jades and African violets can be propagated by rooting a single leaf.

To root these cuttings, place them in a clean container filled with moist, porous media such as vermiculite, perlite or potting soil. Cuttings will root in plain water, but the roots will be starved for oxygen and susceptible to root rot.

Enclose the cutting container in a perforated plastic bag to keep humidity high and prevent the plants from wilting. Keep the containers out of direct sunlight until the cuttings have rooted.

There is no need for fertilization during the rooting process, but be sure the media stay moist. Your new plants can be potted in a good quality soil mix as soon as the roots are an inch long.

FRED'S SUPER TIP

Roses are the queens of any summer garden, but many people are intimidated by them and let others enjoy all that royal elegance. Yes, roses do take a lot of work, but with regular care your garden can be as fragrant as any on the block.

So here are a few tips for summer rose care:

Roses need steady watering to bloom and remain healthy. Be sure they receive from one to two inches of water a week. If you are watering by hand, that's five to 10 gallons of water for a big bush and two to three gallons for a miniature.

Hot summer means "blackspot," the persistent fungus that produces yellow foliage dotted with fuzzy black spots. All nurseries have rose fungicides, and you'll never get through a season without them. Adding a few drops of dishwater liquid will help it stick to the bush.

Spider mites love hot dry weather and roses. If they're around, foliage on the lower part of the bush will appear dry and brownish-looking. The mites look like ground pepper.

You can wash mites away with a water wand early in the season, but if that's too difficult, use a commercial miticide.

Thrips, aphids, grasshoppers and Japanese beetles are the other insect pests that infect roses. They can and must be treated with regular use of Sevin and Malathion.

Apply special rose fertilizer every two to four weeks depending on its strength. Water the roses well before applying to prevent root damage. Be sure the fertilizer doesn't come in contact with the leaves, especially in hot weather, because it can burn the plant.

A layer of mulch from three to five inches thick is necessary to keep roses in form. Use pine bark, needles, oak leaves or newspapers.

Roses that are kept neatly pruned will consistently produce more flowers than bushes allowed to run wild. Cut the cane just a few inches below the faded bloom, and you will be rewarded with more flowers.

Many rose gardeners also remove most of the foliage at the lower end of the plant to improve air circulation and deprive spider mites of a place to roost.

Be consistent. This sounds like a lot of work because it is. But the fragrant rewards are well worth it.

NOTES

JULY

JULY CHECKLIST

EARLY

- ☐ Don't side-dress sweet potatoes.
- ☐ Fertilize hot peppers and okra.
- ☐ Spray magnolias for sassafras weevils.
- ☐ Check beans for bean leaf rollers.
- ☐ Pinch back, fertilize and mulch mums.
- ☐ Spray for Japanese beetles.
- ☐ Cut roses to take indoors.
- ☐ Cut day lilies for bouquets.
- ☐ Water ferns with a weak tea to replace acidity.
- ☐ Check for striped cucumber beetles and spotted cucumber beetles.
- ☐ Get rid of any squash infected with blossom-end rot.
- ☐ Check peach and nectarine trees for borers.

MIDDLE

- ☐ Thoroughly water trees and shrubs every week.
- ☐ Raise blade on lawn mower and change the oil.
- ☐ Clean out garden and plant fall crops.
- ☐ Remove seed pods and faded flowers from annuals.
- ☐ Check houseplants set outdoors.
- ☐ Water and fertilize indoor houseplants.
- ☐ Dig and divide iris.
- ☐ Check squash plants for squash-vine borer.
- ☐ Check lawn for white grubs.
- ☐ Plan yard renovation.
- ☐ Start biennials indoors to be transplanted to the garden in the fall.
- ☐ Mulch lima beans and check for Mexican bean beetles.
- ☐ Fertilize summer-flowering bulbs.
- ☐ Mulch, water and side-dress tomatoes.
- ☐ Check for azalea lace bug.
- ☐ Dig and divide day lilies.
- ☐ Check evergreens for bagworms.
- ☐ Set traps for moles.

LATE

- ☐ Check for parasitic dodder.
- ☐ Check lawn for whitish-gray slime.
- ☐ Check garden for sow bugs.
- ☐ Check for whiteflies.
- ☐ Check apple, pear and crab-apple trees for signs of fire blight.
- ☐ Water and fertilize fuchsias and check for whiteflies and spider mites.

SUPER TIP

- ☐ When to harvest your crops.

July is more of June, only worse. The heat is getting a little tougher to take, and the garden is just as demanding. Still, there are those quiet nights, when the sun dips down below the trees and you are alone with your sweet corn, green beans, early potatoes and late-evening thoughts, that it all seems worthwhile.

July was named for — and this shouldn't surprise you by now — Julius Caesar. July was first named Quintilis, which means fifth, because it once was the fifth month. But Julius Caesar made it seventh, and the Roman senate went along with it by naming the month Julius — which became July — in honor of him. Roman senates could do that kind of stuff.

The average high temperature in Kentuckiana in July is 87.6 degrees; the average low 67.5. The average monthly precipitation is 4.10 inches, but in 1875, a record year, 16.46 inches of rain fell in Louisville. The lowest July rainfall was .25 inches, which fell, sorta, in 1930.

July thunderstorms left their mark in Lexington, where on July 3, 1931, 1.54 inches of rain fell in 15 minutes, and in Louisville, where 2.66 inches fell in 30 minutes on July 18, 1971.

As absolutely miserable as the summer of 1988 was overall, its July readings of 103 degrees still didn't set a record for the month. That pleasure went to July 24, 1901, July 28, 1930, and July 14, 1936, when the temperature hit 107 degrees in Louisville. The lowest July temperature ever was 49 degrees on July 24, 1947.

The hottest day ever in Indi-ana was the 116 degrees registered in Collegeville on July 14, 1936.

And the hottest day ever in Kentucky? On July 28, 1930, the thermometer hit 114 degrees in Greensburg in Green County.

There are 14 hours and 47 minutes of sun on July 1, and 14 hours and 10 minutes on July 31 as the growing seasons begins to creep away toward the west. The average soil temperature is between 77 and 85 degrees.

P.T. Barnum, a man who knew his nuts and bananas, was born on July 5, 1810, and author Henry Thoreau, who moved to the edge of Walden Pond to write of man and nature, was born July 12, 1817.

EARLY

Now that early July has arrived, here's something you should NOT being doing: fertilizing or side-dressing your sweet potatoes.

Sweet potatoes love hot weather, but too much fertilizer, especially nitrogen, will produce long, thin fruit that look like sweet pencils. So remember to water, and you can trim back the vines a little if they grow too wild, but they don't need fertilizer.

Two vegetables that will profit from warm-weather fertilizing are hot peppers and okra. Give them a 1/4 cup of 10-10-10 fertilizer per 10-foot row and repeat that every four to six weeks. Be sure to keep picking the fruit, too, because if you don't, the plants will pout and quit producing.

Every once in awhile in early summer I get calls from people who want to know what causes the holes in the leaves of their magnolias. The culprit is often the tiny sassafras weevil, which also goes by the alias magnolia leaf miner.

The weevils often feed in early July, then drop to the ground to spend the winter hiding there. You can lay them away permanently now by spraying with Sevin.

Check your beans now for one of the more curious bugs you will ever see — the bean leaf roller. The roller is actually a blue-green caterpillar with a big, black head and a bad attitude. It feeds on bean leaves, which it will neatly cut and fold over to form a tent that would make a Boy Scout happy. If there are not too many of them, they are fun to watch. If they become pests, Sevin will solve the problem.

Mums should be pinched back three or four times during the summer to make them more bushy when show time arrives in the fall. If your plants have become too leggy, try rooting some of the longer clippings in pots and starter soil.

You can also promote better buds in the established plant by using a low-nitrogen fertilizer like 5-10-10. Use 1/2 cup per square yard and be sure to water in the fertilizer. Mulch will also keep mums healthy in the hot summer months.

Japanese beetles, those marauding visitors from the Orient, continue to plague gardeners in our area, sometimes in swarms of hundreds. One local gardener even complained to me that the beetles had devoured her rose garden bush by bush. She said she knew it was the Japanese beetle because it sat there cross-legged on a leaf eating with chopsticks.

The beetle, with its shiny copper-brown body and metallic green head, actually feeds on nearly 300 plants, including shrubs, fruit and shade trees, grape leaves and even larch trees. The beetle damage is easy to spot because the leaves are reduced to skeletons. You can buy Japanese beetle traps, but they often just lure more beetles into the area. The best chemical control is Sevin or Malathion.

Healthy roses can be enjoyed twice this time of year; once in the garden and later indoors. Be sure you cut the roses properly to ensure more flowers. Roses have either three, five or seven leaflets on each stem. Cut the stem so that at least one bunch of five or seven leaflets remains immediately below the cut. This will guarantee more flowers, not just more foliage.

Use a sharp knife, make the cut at an angle and submerge the cut roses in a pail of warm water. Once inside, remove all foliage that will be beneath the water line in the vase. Recut the ends so they will absorb water more readily. Place them in a cool spot, possibly even in the refrigerator, to give them a "rest" before they are set out.

Speaking of cut flowers, the selfless day lily will also make a nice indoor bouquet if handled properly. Cut off a stalk with several buds, place it in warm water and remove the spent flowers as new buds open.

If your fern looks a little peaked these days, try giving it a spot of tea. Yes, that's correct, a spot of tea. Ferns thrive in a peaty-type soil that's high in acid. When we water ferns as often as they like, we often wash a lot of acidity out of the soil,

which can be replaced with a drink of tea.

Just drop a tea bag in two quarts of water and pour it on the fern. I do this once or twice a year, especially when the fern fronds begin to turn a light green.

Oh yes, when it comes to pouring tea on your ferns, remember: They drink it straight up. Skip the cream and sugar.

Stay on guard against the striped cucumber beetle and the spotted cucumber beetle. They carry the bacteria that produces bacterial wilt, the leading cause of sudden death among cucumbers, cantaloupes and melons. The beetles can be controlled with Sevin, methoxychlor, Rotenone or diazinon if used every seven to 10 days.

Gardeners often call in early July to ask why their squash are rotting at one end. The problem is a disease called "blossom-end rot," which is different from the fungus of the same name that attacks tomatoes. With squash, the rot comes in the form of a grayish mold that begins at the blossom and consumes the whole plant. It's caused by hot, humid weather and uneven watering. There is no cure. Pick off all infected squash and throw them away.

The backyard peach or nectarine tree is often susceptible to borers that will girdle the tree, killing it. The borers are active all summer but can be controlled with a spray or "painting" of Thiodan about July 1, as well as Aug. 1 and Sept. 1. Mark those dates on your calendar.

If you find the leaves of some vegetables — like eggplants or tomatoes — mysteriously disappearing, look around for the blister beetle. It's black and gray, about 1/2 inch long, and will chew leaves until it defoliates the whole plant. It can be controlled with Rotenone or methoxychlor. The good news is that the bug's babies feed on grasshopper eggs. The bad news is that it's called a blister beetle because its juices, as a defense mechanism, will cause blisters on your skin.

MIDDLE

We won't forget the drought of 1988 for a long, long time. It caused damage to flowers, trees and shrubs that may haunt us for several years because the heat could have severely weakened many plants, especially newly planted ones. In fact, plants that barely make it through a severe drought may die the following winter, especially if the winter is severe. Keep that in mind if some of your shrubs mysteriously refuse to come alive next spring.

That's why it's more important than ever to water weekly all summer unless Mother Nature does it for you. For smaller trees, let the hose run for 15 to 20 minutes to give them a good soaking. Don't just lay the hose against the trunk. The roots extend as least as far as the tree's drip line and possibly twice that far, so move the hose around.

During the hot summer

months, be sure to raise the blade on your lawn mower about an inch. This will allow the plants to grow strong and form roots. If you haven't had the lawn-mower blades sharpened since spring, they're way overdue.

There's also a good chance you have 600 pounds of caked grass under the mower deck, and the mower might even need an oil change, a chore many homeowners tackle about once every 36 months. Take care of your mower, and it will take care of you.

If you haven't started that fall garden yet, you've still got time. Remove all the old crops and clean out all debris and weeds. Water the garden thoroughly and allow it to dry so it's not muddy. Next, apply one pound of 10-10-10 or 12-12-12 fertilizer per 100 square feet of planting area. If the previous crop grew well, you may not need much more fertilizer. You can plant all the same warm-weather crops you planted in the spring. Refer to the chart we have in this book for suggested planting dates, but remember, those are just rough dates; no two years are the same.

One trick for increasing germination in warm weather is to dig a furrow and flood it with water two or three times. Then sow the seeds in the furrow and cover them with the soil you removed. Water will rise from the lower soil levels by capillary action and keep the seeds moist for several days. After a few days, resume normal watering.

Continue to pick faded flowers and seed pods from your annuals, especially marigolds, cosmos, snapdragons and zinnias. Cut all the long, scraggly stems off your petunias. Use a fungicide to control powdery mildew on zinnias and phlox. If your salvia are looking bleak and faded, trim off the old flowers with clippers. The plant will produce new ones by fall, and they'll be especially bright in the cooler weather.

Be sure to check daily on houseplants set outside for the summer. They can be severely damaged in just one long day of heat. It often helps in hot weather to dig a trench and bury the pots to protect the sensitive roots.

Houseplants are also susceptible to insect attacks and mildew. Those plants in clay pots might need watering twice a day. While you're at it, keep an eye on the houseplants you left indoors. They need regularly watering — and fertilizer too.

Irises that haven't been divided in five or six years can be dug, divided and replanted before Aug. 1. It sometimes helps to dip the plants in a bucket of water before dividing them to make them more pliable. It's also time to divide Oriental poppies and bleeding hearts, but only after the foliage dies back.

Check your squash plants for the squash-vine borer, a white, grublike caterpillar that bores into the fruit by tunneling through the vine. Unfortunately, the first sign of the borer is a sudden wilting of an apparently healthy runner. If the vine is infested, the best answer is to slit the stem and kill the borer with a wire. But it can be controlled with regular use of methoxychlor, Thiodan or Rotenone.

The end of July and August are the months to apply Dursban or diazinon to your lawn to control horrible white grubs that produce June beetles, bugs that are also known, somewhat mysteriously, as masked chafers. For best results, mow the lawn, rake out the dead grass and water down the soil immediately after the treatment. Be sure to follow the directions on the package.

While you're at it, walk around your yard and consider whether it needs serious renovation. The renovation is best done from late August to mid-September, but you'll need to make plans now.

July is a good month to start biennials such as hollyhocks, foxglove, honesty, wallflowers and Canterbury bells from seed indoors. The seedlings will be big enough to transplant outdoors this fall, and you'll have great flowers next spring.

You may not like to sit out under a hot summer sun, but your lima beans love it. But they are extremely sensitive to root injury when in bloom, so applying mulch in July is very beneficial. If you side-dress with fertilizer between the time the flowers bloom and the pods form, you'll not get the best fruit. Use Sevin to control the Mexican bean beetle.

Your summer flowering bulbs such as lilies should be in bloom now. They can be helped with a light dusting of 5-10-10 or 10-10-

10 fertilizer but avoid a high-nitrogen fertilizer because it can cause bulb decay. As the flowers fade, cut them off to prevent seed formation.

Remember, tomatoes, the vegetable gardeners most like to brag about, are susceptible to a bushelbasket full of problems in hot weather. Tomatoes will suffer blossom-end rot, cracked skin, sunscald and leaf roll. The trick to avoiding these ills is even watering, mulching and side-dressing with ammonium nitrate after the fruit has set. Scatter one tablespoon in a 6- to 10-inch circle around each plant. Repeat every two weeks.

It's time to keep a sharp eye out for the azalea lace bug, a pest that despite its aristocratic name can cut some real blue-collar holes in your azaleas and rhododendrons. So if the leaves of your plants are spotted and have brownish specks on the underside, it's time to spray them with Malathion or Sevin. With a severe infestation, it might take two or three applications seven days apart. And keep watering those azaleas and rhododendrons, especially the newly planted ones; they have very shallow root systems.

I've often called day lilies the lazy man's flower because they aren't fussy about sun, water or fertilizer and aren't bothered by insects or diseases. They are called day lilies because each individual flower only lasts one day. They should be dug and divided every four or five years, and the best time to do that is

right after they are finished blooming — right about now.

Use a very sharp shovel and replant the clumps to the same depth. Dipping the plants in a bucket of water will also help in dividing day-lily clumps.

While you're at it, be on the lookout for the newer variety of day lilies that will bloom all summer. They're just coming onto the market.

Continue to look for the pesky bagworms, which will be hanging from your evergreens like Christmas tree ornaments. They especially like arborvitae and junipers. Pick them off, or use Sevin or Malathion.

Moles continue to be the greatest pest to homeowners since the door-to-door brush salesman. Most home remedies, from putting used chewing gum in the runs to planting castor beans, are totally without merit. The only sure method is the use of mole traps, which are sold at hardware stores and nurseries.
Good Luck!

LATE

The lovevine is at it again, making passes at all kinds of plants in the garden.

Lovevine is a common name for a parasitic annual called dodder. It looks like a very thin golden-colored string that winds itself around plants and chokes them to death. It's also called, less poetically, "strangleweed" and "goldthread."

There is no chemical way to discourage this lover of garden plants. The only way is to sit down and untangle it by hand. Take a stool to the garden with you. There are less pleasant ways to spend a summer evening. To insure the lovevine's demise, apply a pre-emergent weed control to the infected area late next spring.

In the warm, moist days of late July you may begin to notice slimy circles of mold from 1 to 24 inches in diameter forming on your lawn. Usually whitish-gray, but sometimes even yellow or red, slime mold looks ugly and permanent.

Fortunately, just like the Wicked Witch in the "Wizard of Oz," the slime can be easily washed away with a good splashing of water. Throw it from a bucket, like Dorothy did, or just use the garden hose.

People often call or write asking about those gray, tank-like garden bugs that hide in shady, damp places and roll up like a ball when disturbed. They are sow bugs, also called "pillbugs," and are actually members of the crab and lobster family.

Sow bugs feed on organic matter in the soil but also like the tender roots of plants and flowers. They can be controlled with diazinon, but an organic gardener I know eliminates them with orange peels. He places sections of the rind — he saves the fruit for himself — all through his vegetable garden, especially in cool, damp places.

The sow bugs collect on the rinds at night, and in the day the gardener picks them up and kills them in boiling water.

My grandfather used to call whiteflies "flying dandruff." They are the tiny, whitish insects which congregate under many leaves, especially those of tomato plants, and fly in great clouds from one plant to another when disturbed.

Orthene, Thiodan and insecticidal soap will control them. But since the flies are attracted to the color yellow, an organic way to get rid of them is to paint a board yellow, then coat it with a tacky substance, even motor oil. The whiteflies head for the yellow and get stuck. It's the 10-W-40 way to bug control.

Blackened twigs and branches on your apple, pear or crab-apple trees indicate they have fire blight. It will spread if not checked, so cut off the limbs below the infected area and destroy them. Be sure to disinfect the pruning tool between each cutting by dipping it in a solution of bleach and water; otherwise you will spread the disease. Spraying this time of year does not help.

Remember those fuchsias you bought this spring because they looked so cool, clean and pretty? Well, they will not survive the summer without daily watering and a high-phosphorous food like 2-10-10 fertilizer. They also attract whiteflies and spider mites the way the ice-cream man attracts kids, so treat the insects with Orthene, Thiodan or insecticidal soap.

What the heck, treat the kids to ice cream too.

FRED'S TIPS

Are the squirrels and birds getting to your sweet corn before you do? One trick is to wait until the corn is done dropping pollen, then cover the ears with paper sandwich bags, or the plastic grocery store bags. The ears will develop inside the bags.

I know a gardener in Frankfort, Ky., who uses feet cut from old pantyhose to stop marauders. Sometimes squirrels can nudge off a paper bag, but they can't remove pantyhose.

When harvesting corn, the ears should be snapped off the stalk with a downward push, twist and pull. Keep practicing the motion, and you might also develop a big-league curve ball.

Your pets are also bothered by insects — particularly fleas — during the hot summer months. They should be taken to the vet for regular checks and baths, but you should also be dusting them with powders and lotions available at pet stores.

The best way to water bigger

trees and shrubs is with a special "soaker hose." They may cost a little more but are worth it because they allow the water to slowly seep into the ground. With a regular hose, the water may rush away from the tree roots and be wasted.

You'll get the most nutritional value from many vegetables — and often the best taste — by eating them raw. This includes peas, beans, summer squash, cauliflower, broccoli and even sweet corn. When you do cook them, try using as little water as possible. A vegetable "steamer" is the best.

While an insecticide will do some good even after the bugs have arrived, fungicides are different; they must be on the plant as a protective layer BEFORE disease strikes. They can't do anything to prevent disease once it has hit. Don't give up if you see evidence of disease; the fungicide can prevent future damage. But it can't cure what's already sick — or dead.

My wife and I raise quite a sizeable planting of blueberries each year, and I'm proud to say that we — not the birds — get all the crop. Our Save Our Blueberries (SOB) method involves metal rods used for electric fence, white PVC pipe and a roll of fruit-tree netting. I stake the metal rods along both sides of the patch, then use the hollow, bendable PVC pipe inserted on the rods to form arches. We secure netting to the PVC pipe with twist ties and leave enough netting at each end to use as flaps, which we secure with clothespins.

The type of arrangement you use will depend on the size of the crop you are protecting, but the same materials should work for a variety of berries that the birds like to share with man.

Rosie Lerner, a Purdue University extension horticulturist, says that a lemon-lime carbonated beverage makes a good homemade floral preservative. Lemon-lime pop provides citric acid to help prevent bacterial growth. It also provides sugar, which the flower loses as it ages. Do not use the beverage alone. Dilute it by half with water. Cut the flowers in early morning or late evening to get the maximum amount of water in the plant. Please, please, don't drink the water.

Those family photographs taken in the yard may be more valuable than you think. Landscape plants can add 25 percent to the market value of a house, and house damage caused by a falling tree may be covered by insurance. So while you're taking pictures, move around the yard, document every tree over six inches in height and store the pictures in a dark safety-deposit box next to the $1.5 million in cash. The pictures will help in making a claim.

Now that we're well into harvest season, why not keep a list — just for one week — of the amount of vegetables you take from your garden. Next time you go to the store, check the prices. It might be fun to see how much

money your garden has saved you.

If your garden is plagued by continuous rainfall for several days, you can help the soil dry out by walking through the garden with a hoe or spading fork and opening the soil so the water can drain away. Just poking holes in the soil can help.

You'd think eggplant has feelings, and in a sense it does; it is very sensitive to cold water. To keep eggplant from sulking, keep it well-supplied with water that's had a chance to sit in the sun for a time. Often the water will warm up just being inside a hose out in the sun.

Cannas are tough enough to survive with little care and plenty of water. But they'll keep blooming longer if you remove the old flowering stalk just above the first set of leaves. Use sharp shears, and a new flower will bloom below the cut. To keep the plants lush, fertilize every few weeks with a 10-10-10 fertilizer. Dusting with Sevin will keep the leaf-roller caterpillar at bay.

Hostas, which like their shade, also respond very well to watering. A friend of mine has one growing in the shade near a downspout, and it's twice the size of any other. It produces better, and more fragrant, blossoms in early September, too.

If you divide your crowded Boston fern plants now, they'll fill out again by the end of the summer. Use a knife to divide the tough rootball into several sections. Plant each section in a suitable-sized pot and keep well-watered. Feed once a month during the summer. Use a water-soluble fertilizer like 18-18-18.

Some people occasionally try to rid their yards of poison ivy by burning it. Burning may work, but don't stand in the smoke. It can spread the poison just as readily as physical contact. Remember: To kill the weed, you must dig up the whole root system. Chemical control with Kleenup or Amitrol requires repeated applications.

If you think you touched the plant, wash the affected area with lukewarm water and a strong, alkaline laundry detergent. Then find some calamine lotion or hydrocortisone cream.

If you want to protect your indoor houseplants while you're on vacation, water them well, let the soil drain, and wrap the plants in a black plastic bag. That will prevent the soil from drying too quickly. Be sure to keep the bags out of direct sunlight.

If you're going to be gone for several weeks, trust your plants to a good, reliable neighbor. There aren't enough plastic bags in the world to replace one good neighbor.

FRED'S SUPER TIP

One thing many gardeners need to know is exactly when to harvest their crops, especially sweet corn and melons. Here's a brief list of the more popular crops:

Sweet corn should be picked when the kernels are milky. Pull back the shuck and squeeze a kernel with your fingernail. If the liquid is watery, the corn is not ready. If there's no liquid, it's ready for cattle feed. If it's milky, it's ready for the dinner table.

One other thing: The good gardener wears track shoes into the garden patch. Sweet corn should be in the kitchen to be cooked and served no longer than 9.8 seconds after it has been picked.

July and August are the months to harvest the onions you want to keep through the winter. The best time to harvest is when about half the tops have dried and fallen over. Waiting too long increases the chances of sunburn and decay. Use a spading fork to work the onions loose, let them dry in a dry, well-ventilated area for 10 to 12 days and store them in a cool, dry place.

Harvest cucumbers for slicing when they are at least three inches long, firm and have a good green color. If you plan to make pickles, harvest cucumbers when they are two to four inches long for sweet pickles, four to six inches long for dill pickles.

Green beans are most tender when the seed inside the pod is about one-third full size or begins to show through the pod. As the beans mature, the pods get more stringy.

Tomatoes should be evenly red but still firm to the touch. If you pick a day or two early, let them ripen at room temperature, but not in a sunny window. Do not store tomatoes in a refrigerator as it adversely affects the taste.

Begin to harvest beets when they are a little more than an inch in diameter and try to get the rest before they exceed three inches. Any bigger and they get pithy. Beet greens make good eating and can be harvested when the tops are big enough for cooking.

If you've been thinning carrots all along — and you should have been — you'll find that the longer they are in the ground, the tougher they become. In general — and carrots vary greatly in size and diameter — just pick them when they're the size you like to eat. Baby carrots are really yummy.

Dig potatoes when the tops yellow and die back. High soil temperatures can cause overripening. Avoid leaving spuds out in the sunlight. Baby potatoes can be dug by early July or several weeks after the plants have reached full growth. They are often the tastiest then. Be careful not to bruise the fruit.

Eggplant is edible from the time it is 1/3 grown until ripe and bright with color. Use it quickly because eggplant doesn't store well.

Pumpkins and winter squash should be harvested before the first frost, when the skin is hard and the colors darken. To avoid spoilage, do not pile them on top of each other.

Muskmelons should be harvested at the "full slip" stage, which loosely translates to the time when the plant will slip easily from the vine. However, the serious gardener must also solemnly "thump" the fruit to determine if it sounds ready.

Harvest green peppers when they are firm. If you want red peppers, just let them hang out there until the peppers turn red. Be sure to cut the peppers off the bush to save injury and to keep more peppers coming.

Sweet potatoes can be dug anytime the tubers seem large enough. But they are very susceptible to frost, so a good trick is to cut away all the vines after the crop has fully matured. Since the vines often cover about 56 acres, it makes the digging much easier too.

Watermelons can be taken into the kitchen when the underside turns from whitish to creamy yellow, the rind losses its gloss and appears dull, the stem dries up and the melon yields a dull "thud" when hit. If your hand goes into the melon to the third knuckle, you've got a problem. Another sure-fire method is to cut a "plug" from the melon and taste it when nobody is looking. Just be sure to put it back for another day.

NOTES

AUGUST

AUGUST CHECKLIST

EARLY
- ☐ Water tomatoes and apply fungicides and insecticides.
- ☐ Check for powdery mildew.
- ☐ Cultivate cantaloupes with care.
- ☐ Sharpen lawn-mower blade and change oil; also, change pattern of mowing.
- ☐ Continue watering lawn.
- ☐ Fertilize amaryllis and snip off buds after blooms are gone.
- ☐ Remove old and rotting fruit from garden.
- ☐ Check beans for rust.
- ☐ Stop spraying fruit trees two weeks before harvest.
- ☐ Begin transforming luffa gourd into a sponge.
- ☐ Begin fall garden.

MIDDLE
- ☐ Cultivate night-blooming cereus.
- ☐ Do not fertilize trees and shrubs.
- ☐ Harvest grapes two to three weeks after color change.
- ☐ Decide what kind of bulbs to order to be planted in the fall.
- ☐ Prune and destroy all raspberry and blackberry canes that bore fruit.
- ☐ Take cuttings from annuals to start plants that will overwinter indoors.
- ☐ Pick dead buds off bedding plants to keep the plants blooming.

LATE
- ☐ Harvest pears when fruit changes color.
- ☐ Continue checking trees for bagworms and tent caterpillars.
- ☐ Plant "green-manure" crop to improve garden soil.
- ☐ If winter squash are ready, pick them and cure them in the sun.
- ☐ Have someone mow your lawn while you're away on vacation.
- ☐ Don't prune landscape plants.
- ☐ Keep evergreens, trees and azaleas well-watered.

SUPER TIP
- ☐ Patching your lawn.

August, with all its heat and droning crickets, brings us state fairs and a time to celebrate all that we have grown. It's the time when we become aware that the world has begun to reverse itself; the days are shorter, the nights are longer, and the occasional touch of autumn air is refreshing against the skin.

August was named for the great Roman leader Augustus, but the matter didn't stop there. That same Roman senate that named the month for Augustus stole a day from February and tacked it onto August to make the calendar work better. Don't you wish you could do that on Monday morning?

The average high temperature in Kentuckiana in August is 86.7 degrees, down slightly from July. The average low is 66.1 degrees. The average rainfall is 3.31 inches. Dry spells are common, but on one memorable August day, Aug. 29, 1917, .79 inches of rain fell on Louisville in just five minutes. That would have totaled 9.48 inches in one hour had it continued.

The record rainfall for the month was 10.53 inches, set in 1888. Seven years previous, in 1881, there was only .15 inches of rain, a record for the driest August.

The summer of '88 didn't break the all-time record for the single hottest day in August either. It reached 101 one day in August 1988, but it was 105 on Aug. 12, 1881, and on Aug. 5, 1918. The coldest August day ever was 45 degrees on Aug. 31, 1946.

There are 14 hours and eight minutes of sun on Aug. 1, and 13 hours and four minutes on Aug. 31. The average soil temperature ranges from 77 to 84 degrees.

William Clark, a leader of the Louis and Clark expedition and the brother of local hero George Rogers Clark, was born Aug. 1, 1770. The United States annexed Hawaii on Aug. 12, 1898, guaranteeing us good pineapples forever.

EARLY

It's normal for tomatoes to stop producing when the temperature rises into the 90s and stays there. It's just so doggone hot in these "dog days" that the pollen gums up and becomes infertile. Keep watering and applying fungicides and insecticides. There will be more tomatoes later.

Powdery mildew and August often go hand in glove, or mildew on leaf, as the case may be. Mildew is the powdery, grayish-white stuff you see on dahlias, honeysuckle, lilacs, privet, roses and zinnias. It arrives in August because it often overwinters in the Deep South, and its spores are blown northward every spring and summer.

Mildew thrives on evenings with heavy dew. To fight it, soak the soil when watering rather than sprinkling the foliage. Then buy a mildew fungicide containing sulfur. Benlate is a good one, but it must be used every 10 to 14 days. It can't save what's been infected, but it can protect what's left.

One year while mowing around the garden I saw a cantaloupe wobbling along the plant leaves. I thought the heat of the day was getting to me. I tiptoed up to the quaking melon . . . and there, sticking out from the far side of the melon, was the back end of a well-fed box turtle.

From then on I placed the melons on top of old flower pots as they neared maturity, and that seemed to eliminate the problem.

Also remember this: Cantaloupe vines have shallow roots and should be cultivated with care. Lifting the vines unnecessarily — except when charging box turtles are around — may reduce production by interfering with pollination.

By now you've probably logged about 10,000 foot miles behind the trusty lawn mower. It may be time to sharpen the blade again and change the oil. Also, try cutting the yard in different patterns for the rest of the summer. It will help break the monotony, and it's better for the grass if you cut it at different angles and from different directions. You'll get a whole new perspective on life, come up with a great idea and make $10 million. Just send me 10 percent.

We've talked about the importance of regular watering, but if you still need help, here's a formula I've found that will help you decide how much water you need:

If your garden hose is 1/2 inch in diameter, let the water run for about an hour to get the equivalent of one inch of rain. If your hose is 5/8 inch, let it run 37 minutes. If your hose is 3/4 inch, it will take only 24 minutes.

The type of sprinkler you use, of course, is a factor in this. To double-check, place a can under the spray and watch the clock. When there's an inch of water in the can, you'll know how long the sprinkler should run.

A man called me one day in August to report the strangest sight he had ever seen; a stalk had emerged from the ground near his house and on top of it was a large clump of lily-like flowers.

"What," he asked, "is that?"

The answer is the "magic lily," the "resurrection lily," or, more interestingly, the "naked lady." The plant is actually an amaryllis that emerges from bulbs that should be planted in the fall.

The man who called had forgotten that the heavy, straplike green leaves that emerged early in the spring and died back were also part of the plant's growth cycle. That leafy orchestra was the first announcement of the plant to come.

Magic lilies will do well in full sun or partial shade. They are extremely hardy and reproduce readily. They should be planted five inches deep and eight inches apart. After the blooms are gone, snip off the buds and fertilize.

As we near the end of the gardening season, it's essential to remove all old and rotting fruit from your garden. It provides the perfect nursery for next year's crop of insects and disease. Keep your garden clean as you go, and it will make the big, year-end cleanup much easier. It also keeps more crops coming this season.

Watch your late-summer beans for a disease called rust, which often makes its first appearance as we head toward Labor Day. It is found most commonly on mature beans having a dense canopy. Look for reddish-brown spots on lower leaf surfaces and pods. It's spread by wind and with garden tools. Fungicides like Maneb or sulfur dust will keep it under control. Begin spraying soon.

Discontinue spraying your fruit trees two weeks before harvest to avoid having poisonous residue on the food. Be sure to check the pesticide or fungicide labels for specific intervals while you are spraying.

Now is the time to begin transforming your luffa gourd into what the pioneers used it for — a sponge. The luffa is a gourd that grows almost two feet in length. It can be eaten like a zucchini or cucumber when young, but as it matures its color turns from green to yellow, which means it's ready to pick.

First, soak the gourd in water until the skin peels away and a fibrous skeleton is left — that's the sponge. Remove the seeds for next year's crop and let the sponge dry in the sun for a day. After it has cured, wash it thoroughly and take it to the kitchen. You'll find it is very stiff and coarse, but it will make an excellent pot-scrubber and conversation piece.

In Japan luffas are used for shoe soles, filters and pillow stuffings. In Europe they are used in health spas and for bathing. I tried that once and didn't like it. It was like bathing with a scouring pad.

It's still not too late to begin a fall garden of warm-weather crops, including bush beans, carrots, beets and transplants of cabbage, cauliflower and broccoli — if you can find them. It's a little early yet to plant lettuce, mustard greens, spinach and turnips in a fall garden. They don't like the heat. Late August or early September is a better time for them.

MIDDLE

The peace and tranquillity of a good night's sleep in mid-August was broken a few years ago by the sound of the telephone ringing. The caller was excited.

"My plant," she said. "You must come see it."

"At midnight?" I said. "Can't it wait until morning?"

But I knew the answer was no, because her plant was the night-blooming cereus. It's an unusual member of the cactus family, with broad, leathery leaves that narrow to a point at the top.

Once a year, usually in mid-summer, older cereus plants put out magnificent, water-lilylike flowers; white with purple on the outer petals. To get one to bloom, you need porous, well-drained soil and eternal vigilance with the water; the plant must be kept moist all summer. It needs soil on the dry side in winter, with a bright location and temperatures at 40 to 45 degrees.

Is the night-blooming cereus rare? Not judging by the number of late-blooming phone calls I get.

So if you have one and it's getting ready to bloom, do me a favor; don't call me, I'll call you.

Given the hot weather in mid- to late August, you may be tempted to fertilize your droopy-looking trees and shrubs to pep them up. DON'T do it. A belt of fertilizer now could stimulate growth that won't have time to harden off by winter and will probably be killed by cold weather. You don't want to fertilize again until late in the fall, after the first freeze has stopped growth or the leaves have dropped. Fertilizer then will help the tree roots get ready for next year.

Your grapes have changed color by now, either to red, or purple, or possibly a different shade of green than they were initially. But most cultivars shouldn't be harvested until two to three weeks after the color change to give them time to fully ripen. The grapes may look ready to eat before then, but they are not.

It's time to begin searching the catalogs for the tulip, daffodil, crocus and other bulbs you'll want blooming in your garden next spring. But it's way too early to plant them now. If you did, they could sprout prematurely in the warm weather, using up all the gusto they need for next spring. Look over the catalogs and order now, but be patient; most bulb companies don't ship until planting time anyway.

While you're waiting, draw a map of exactly where you want each bulb. Be creative. Have fun. You might even work the soil and add a little fertilizer to get it ready.

If you haven't done it yet, be sure to prune and destroy all the raspberry and blackberry canes that bore fruit this year. They will not produce fruit again but could produce disease. It helps to thin out the patch, and you can get an idea of what you'll have next year by seeing what's left.

It's time to take cuttings from annuals such as impatiens, coleus, geraniums and wax begonias to start some plants that will over-winter indoors. Be sure to pick new, healthy growth. Use sharp shears. Use a root fertilizer and place the cuttings in vermiculite, perlite or peat moss rather than water. Keep them moist and in bright, indirect light while they get started. They need the very best treatment this time of year.

From our Where Have You Heard This Before Dept. comes another reminder: Keep picking the buds off the bedding plants to keep them flowering. Keep removing the crops from the garden to keep the plants producing. It's too easy to neglect all that in the heat of August. If they look too sickly, trim off all the tops. Most will rejuvenate for a fall show.

LATE

If you're lucky enough to have a pear tree, remember that pears ripen best off the tree. Harvest them when the fruit turns from a dark green to a lighter green but before they get to an overripe, screaming yellow. Set the pears in a cool, dry, brightly lit place, and they'll be edible in just a few days.

Continue to hand-pick bagworms and look for or any tent caterpillars that might have set up homemaking in the crotches of your trees. You may need shears to cut out the homes of the caterpillars. Their nests can be burned, or you can kill the pests with Sevin, provided you tear a hole in the bag first. Be sure to hunt them late in the day when all the caterpillars have crawled back into their tents.

One of the most reliable methods of improving poor garden soil is to plant a "green-manure" cover crop. This adds organic matter to the soil and, depending on the cover crop used, it also helps add nitrogen to the soil.

The type of "cover crop" you should consider includes hairy vetch, burr clover, soybeans, cowpeas and sorghums.

Most cover crops are legumes; that is, their roots have nitrogen-fixing nodules that extract nitrogen from the air and put it in the soil. You should sow the green-manure crop in early fall, let it grow into the winter, then plow it under four to eight weeks before you are ready to plant.

If your winter squash is ready to pick now, you planted it too soon. You want to harvest winter squash about Oct. 1. The flavor is usually better then because cold weather increases the sugar content.

If they must be picked now — and most green winter squash varieties are ready when they get some strong brown, yellow or bronze color to them — cure them in the sun and store them where it's 55 to 60 degrees.

But if you had planted them about July 1, you wouldn't have this problem. It's summer squash, like zucchini, that should be planted in May.

I saw a cartoon recently that showed a family returning from vacation. A small boy got out of the car and was standing in grass over his head. He turned to his father and said, "Hey, Dad, you forgot to turn off the grass."

Alas, the grass doesn't turn off. Before leaving for vacation, even in August, be sure that someone will cut the lawn. It's better for the grass and provides more security for your home.

Don't do any heavy pruning of landscape plants now. They are getting ready for winter and don't need any ends exposed. It could lead to death from a cold. When winter gets here you can prune some hollies, magnolias or evergreens for Christmas foliage, but do it carefully because those cuttings will leave a "hole" in the plant.

It's especially important that you keep your evergreen trees, azaleas and rhododendrons well-watered in the fall in order to get them through the winter. They often have shallow roots and are more susceptible to drying out than other trees.

FRED'S TIPS

Most insecticides contain a substance that helps them stick to the plants in the rain. If you get an inch or more of rain, however, chances are the insecticide has been washed away. But that still doesn't mean the food is safe to eat. Always observe the time listed on the chemical that specifies the days between application and harvest. You'll have to reapply after a heavy rain.

Fall webworms are those green or yellow insects that spin a web over the ends of branches and turn the leaves inside into skeletons. The web is then extended to take in fresh foliage. The webs can be cut off and burned, or the webworms can be killed with Sevin or Malathion, but you must open the bag for the spray to penetrate.

Webworms are often confused with tent caterpillars, which usually live in the crotches of trees. Some webworms particularly like flowering crabs.

The age-old way of preserving herbs is to dry them by hanging the bouquets in a well-ventilated, dust-free room. If the air is dusty, or if the herbs have seeds that may fall, the herbs can be hung in bunches in brown paper bags. Just be sure the bag has a lot of holes punched in it for ventilation.

But a newer way to preserve herbs is to freeze them. First, wash the herbs, pat off the excess water, place them in plastic bags and pop them into the freezer as soon as possible. Mint, tarragon, lovage, parsley, chives, sorrel and sweet marjoram can be handled this way. You can just snip off what you need from the frozen herbs.

Another method, according to the U.S. Department of Agriculture, is to put chopped herbs into an ice-cube tray, fill with water and freeze. Store the cubes in a plastic bag and drop them into stews or soups as needed.

Rosemary is a tender herb that can be preserved for the winter by taking a baby plant indoors. It's done by a process called "layering." Take a sharp knife and partially cut through the stem of a rosemary plant where it's still covered with soil. After a few weeks, roots will form at the cut. Then cut the whole rooted shoot from the mother plant and put it in a new pot. Take it indoors, but give it bright light all winter — possibly even adding fluorescent light during the short winter days. It can go back outdoors next spring.

Fall broadleaf-weed control with the use of 2,4-D can only work if the weeds are growing. So try to time the application right after a period of heavy rain. But if you've planted new grass, be sure the grass has been mowed at least twice before applying weedkiller because it could damage the new grass.

I'm always collecting garden ideas from people who listen to my radio or television shows, and here's one to protect grapes from the birds: Use old nylon stockings. Just pull the stockings over your grape bunches and tie both ends. The stockings will expand as the grapes grow, you'll keep the bunches intact, and you can reuse the stockings next year.

Did you know you can use the berries of the pyracantha to make a delicious, orange-colored jelly? The bush, which does have long, sharp needles to protect its crop, bears fruit in late summer.

According to one Purdue University horticulturist, you make the jelly by adding one cup of water to each pound of well-washed berries. Boil the water 20 to 25 minutes.

Drain the mixture into a flannel bag and press out the juice, since that's what you need for the jelly. Mix seven cups of water to three cups of pyracantha juice and add the juice of two lemons. Bring the mixture to a boil and add jelling agent. Pour into sterilized jars and seal with paraffin. Then pop some bread in the toaster next Saturday morning and spread on the jelly.

Here's a tip that may help save a tree that's already been damaged in a heavy windstorm. If a heavy limb has been injured to the extent that it must be removed with a chain saw, make your first cut underneath the limb at the point where the branch meets the bark of the trunk.

Cut through the bark with an upward stroke about 1 inch deep. If you saw through the limb from the top without making the undercut first, there is a good chance the heavy branch will rip the bark off the limb as it falls.

Never leave a stub of the limb on the tree. Cut it off almost flush with the trunk. A stub will only serve as an entry point for insects and disease. Do not use a wound dressing on the cut. If you do, no air can get to the wound, and it will fester.

FRED'S SUPER TIP

From now until mid-September is the best time to walk every inch of the lawn looking for bare spots, mole runs, weedy areas and weak turf. Rent a dethatcher from your lawn center to sweep the lawn of dead grass. If you feel ambitious, an old-fashioned tool called a rake will do much the same thing.

If you plan a major renovation and switch of grass varieties — and that will be covered in depth in September's Super Tip — now is the time to kill out the grass you have with a complete herbicide like Roundup or Kleenup. Please be sure to read all directions carefully. You don't want to kill everything else.

When reseeding thin spots, be sure to use the same type or mixture of grass seed already in your lawn. If you're starting the whole lawn over, however, you might choose a tougher fescue that could require less care. Kentucky bluegrass, ironically enough, isn't considered a particularly good grass around here because of the intense heat and humidity.

Think and plan before any renovation, large or small. You've got several weeks. Remember, it does no good to dump tons of seed on the lawn; it will just end up competing with itself. After seeding, rake the seed lightly into the soil or go over the area again with the dethatcher.

In larger bare spots, use straw to cover the seed. Use one bale per 1,000 square feet, but be warned: There will probably be some oats or wheat seeds in the straw. That's no problem. The oats and wheat will be mowed down with the first cutting.

Daily watering will be necessary if there is no rain. Once the seeds sprout, you must keep them moist until they reach booming adolescence, or all you'll have for your trouble is another bare spot.

Don't mow until the grass has been up and growing for two to three weeks. Then resume normal mowing.

NOTES

SEPTEMBER

SEPTEMBER CHECKLIST

EARLY

☐ Get Christmas cactuses ready to bloom.
☐ Plant container-grown or balled and burlapped trees and shrubs.
☐ Bring houseplants indoors.
☐ Check damage done to trees and shrubs by lawn mower.
☐ Remove old raspberry canes and clean up under apple trees.
☐ Divide day lilies, iris, phlox and peonies.
☐ Fertilize strawberries.
☐ Plant parsley seeds for indoor growing.
☐ Plant turnip seeds.
☐ Dust lilacs, zinnias and phlox for powdery mildew; rake leaves
☐ Check lawn for slime mold and sweep it away.
☐ Take cuttings of impatiens, begonias, coleus and geraniums
☐ Dig potatoes.

MIDDLE

☐ Spray roses for diseases and insects.
☐ Have soil analysis done.
☐ Store leftover vegetable and flower seeds.
☐ Dig up and store tubers and corms from tuberous begonias, gladioluses, dahlias, cannas, caladiums and geraniums.
☐ Pick heads off annual flowers to keep them blooming.
☐ Reduce water and stop fertilizing houseplants.
☐ Plant spring-flowering bulbs in pots for early blooming next season.
☐ Gather dirt and mulch to prepare for mounding around rose plants.
☐ Water trees and shrubs.
☐ Begin harvesting gourds.
☐ Harvest flowers for indoor display.
☐ Divide and replant clumps of hollyhocks, perennial salvia and primroses; also transplant columbine, lenten roses and wallflowers.
☐ Water azaleas, rhododendron and camellias.
☐ Transplant poppies.
☐ Check for "dollar spot."
☐ Start a fall salad garden.

LATE

☐ Plant gooseberries.
☐ Harvest popcorn before first frost.
☐ Prepare garden area or raised bed for spring pea plantings.
☐ Begin preparing poinsettias for putting out red bracts.

SUPER TIP

☐ Sowing great grass.

September, with its clean nights and bright, sunny mornings, is the reward we've earned for living around here in July and August. It's the time when the world wakes from its late-summer slumber to the fresh breezes of autumn and realizes, "Holy cow, I've got to transplant my iris and sow some more grass seed!"

September comes from the Latin word **septem**, meaning "seven." Never mind that it's the ninth month. You should know your Romans better than that. September was the seventh month, but by the time Julius Caesar was finished, it was in the ninth slot, and there it shall stay.

The average high temperature in Kentuckiana in September is 80.6 degrees. The average low is 59.1 degrees. The average precipitation is 3.35 inches. That's another nice thing about this country: Most months — spring to fall — average about one inch of rain a week.

The rainiest September since they started keeping records was in 1979, when 10.49 inches fell. The driest was September 1953, when .27 inches fell.

The hottest September day was Sept. 5, 1954, when it was 104 degrees. The coldest was 33 degrees on Sept. 30, 1949, which could have put a little frost on the pumpkin.

The longest drought in Louisville history ran from Sept. 29, 1924, to Oct. 30, 1924, a period of 32 days without rain. We hit 31 days in the summer of '88.

There are 13 hours and one minute of sun on Sept. 1, and 11 hours and 51 minutes of sun on Sept. 30, so get out the blankets. The average soil temperature ranges from 70 to 77 degrees.

Jesse James, an American desperado who knew some long green when he saw it, was born Sept. 5, 1847, and the Treaty of Paris, which officially ended the Revolutionary War in America, was signed Sept. 3, 1783.

EARLY

Start preparing your Christmas cactuses to bloom by giving them 12 hours of complete darkness and night temperatures no higher than 70 degrees. Cover the plants with a thick bag or cloth, but be careful not to injure the stems. Be sure they receive some indirect sunlight the other 12 hours. Do this for eight weeks to 10 weeks, and the buds will appear.

If you don't want to do all that, constant temperatures of about 55 degrees at night will also stimulate the plants to bloom, but it's not easy to find those temperatures in early September.

Fall is an excellent time to plant many container-grown trees or shrubs or nursery stock that has been balled and wrapped in burlap. Planting bare-root stock during this season is a risky venture because the roots do not have a lot of time to "dig in" before Old Man Winter arrives. You can plant bare-root stock after a couple of hard frosts.

Be sure to dig a hole at least twice as wide as the roots, plant at the same depth the tree or shrub grew in the nursery and water well. Stake the taller trees to keep them from rocking in the wind, or the roots will not settle. Be sure your ties don't cut into the tree. Old hose with wire strung through it works well.

Don't forget to bring in houseplants that were moved outdoors for the summer, especially when the temperature consistently falls below 55 degrees. Gradually decrease the amount of light to keep leaf drop to a minimum. Check for disease and bugs who might want to winter indoors before placing the plants next to other houseplants.

Now that we're easing into the end of the lawn-mower season, take a walk around your lawn and inspect trees and shrubs for lawn-mower "teeth marks" that are often the result of careless mowing.

Good watering and an application of fertilizer after the first frost will help the tree or shrub regain its strength. While your looking, don't be alarmed if your white pines or arborvitaes are browning off in the center and dropping some of their needles. All evergreens shed needles at some time but not all at once as do deciduous varieties.

If you haven't removed the old raspberry canes that bore fruit, you better get moving. All suckers outside the hills and rows should be removed. Be sure to clean up all the fallen fruit and leaves around the apple trees while you're at it. It keeps down the disease.

You still have time to trans-

plant or divide day lilies, iris, phlox and peonies. But remember, peonies don't especially like to be moved and are willing to bloom for 30 to 40 years in the same place if you keep them properly fed and pruned.

Be sure to apply two pounds of ammonium nitrate per 100 square feet of strawberry bed area. Brush the granules off the leaves to avoid damage and water right away. All this will put strawberries in your ice cream next year.

Parsley is a fun and useful herb to grow indoors in the winter, and planting can begin now. I think the key to getting parsley seeds jump-started is to soak them eight to 12 hours in water before planting. After the bath, plant the seeds in a six-inch pot of good soil. Keep them in good light and thin out the seedlings to three sturdy plants. Mist occasionally along with regular watering.

When you harvest parsley for garnishes, salads and soups, cut only the outer leaves so the inner ones can develop.

What is the 15th most popular vegetable and the fourth most valuable in terms of nutrition? Why, of course, it's the turnip!

Turnips are one of the better fall crops. They withstand cold temperatures and can be harvested until the ground freezes. They can be eaten raw or cooked and eaten like potatoes. So plant some now. Broadcast the seeds over a wide area, and as they emerge from the soil, pull some of the younger plants and use the "greens" in a salad. They're great.

When looking around some of the gardens in our area in early September, I often see the leaves of plants like lilacs, zinnias and phlox covered with powdery mildew, a grayish substance. University of Kentucky horticulturists recommend dusting with sulfur, and I've also had good luck with Benlate or benomyl.

Rake up and destroy the leaves at season's end, and next season leave a little more space around the plants, which will improve air circulation and cut down on disease.

September's often warm, moist weather is perfect for the development of "slime mold," a fungus-like substance that turns to a gray or black powder when it dries on a bluegrass lawn. It won't damage the lawn, and it can't be eliminated chemically. It feeds on the thatch or decaying material in the soil. The one thing you can do is take a broom and sweep the slime off the grass. This stops damage to grass blades and prevents slime mold from spreading.

There's still time to take cuttings of impatiens, begonias, coleus and geraniums for next year.

Be sure to cut three to six inches from the healthiest plants for better rooting indoors.

Potatoes can be dug before the skins are tough; they almost melt in your mouth at that stage. But if you want potatoes to keep, it's best to wait until the vines have been dead for about two weeks, which is often this time of year. Avoid digging potatoes in bright sun and don't bruise them. Potatoes can be stored for four to six months, but it takes a temperature of about 40 degrees, high humidity and proper ventilation to keep them.

MIDDLE

Don't neglect your roses. Keep up a regular spray schedule for diseases and insects. Roses need a lot more care later in the season, but for now constant surveillance is what's needed.

If your garden is done for the season — or maybe YOU'RE done for the season — there's one more chore you can do to get next year off to a rolling start: Get a soil sample. Now is the best time to do it because the soil laboratories may not be as busy as they are in the spring. Your county agent can help you.

A good soil analysis is vital to keeping your garden producing in top form, and if lime is needed, fall and early winter is the perfect time to add it.

Place leftover vegetable and flower seeds in tightly sealed jars and store them in a dark, cool, dry place. Many seeds will keep for years, and since manufacturers insist on placing a 10-year supply in some packages, you can save a lot of money.

It's getting close to the time to dig your tuberous begonias, glads, dahlias and cannas, although cannas often bloom gloriously into October when all else is fading.

Gladiolus corms should be dug when the leaves have begun to turn yellow. Caladiums, geraniums and tuberous begonias should be dug before a killing frost. You can digs cannas and dahlias after a light frost, but a heavy frost can kill them because it seeps into their roots.

After digging them up, remove the foliage, leaving a short stub, and let the corms and tubers dry for several days. Store them in dry sand or peat moss in a cool, dry place where they won't freeze. A dusting of fungicide will help, but check them all winter; throw out any that show signs of mold or decay.

Keep picking the heads off your annual flowers. Many will have a sudden revival in the shorter, cooler days of summer and will surprise you with lovely blooms until frost.

Because your indoor plants have to get ready to snooze through the winter, you should water them less frequently and stop fertilizing them. Everybody needs a rest some time.

Although it's only September, now is the best time to plant some spring-flowering bulbs in pots so you can force them to bloom indoors in December and January.

It's easy to do. Plant two or three prime daffodil or tulip bulbs in a pot with their tips just above the soil, moisten the soil a little and place the pot in a refrigerator for 10 to 13 weeks. The bulbs will not bloom unless they're fooled into thinking it's winter and the milk is actually a snowman.

When time is up, place the pot in a cool, sunny location and allow three to four weeks for blooms. It will help spring come faster.

It's too early to mound protective dirt around your rose plants; that shouldn't be done until after the leaves drop and the ground is almost frozen. But you should have the dirt, or whatever you'll use for protection, in place and ready to go. It's no fun to move in cold weather. Don't fertilize your roses anymore; give them time to harden off before the snow hits.

Keep watering the baby trees and shrubs you planted this year but don't fertilize them. Surveys have shown that water in the fall is vital to having healthy trees in the spring. It's especially vital following summers with long droughts.

Check your gourds to see if the stems are brown and have begun to dry. If they have, it's time to harvest. Use a sharp knife or shears, leaving a few inches of stem to avoid bruising the fruit. Gourds should be cured for two weeks in 70- to 80-degree heat to preserve them.

Pumpkins and winter squash can be picked when the rind is hard and fully colored. If you can easily dent the rind with a fingernail, they're not ready. They should be stored in a cool place, or they'll be a pulpy mess before you can carve the first jack-o'-lantern.

Now is the time to harvest flowers such as strawflowers, statice, baby's breath and cockscomb for indoor display. After cutting, hang them upside down in a dry, well-ventilated area to help preserve them.

Although your perennial garden may have almost finished blooming for the year, you can get a good start on next year by dividing and replanting overcrowded clumps of hollyhocks, perennial salvia and primroses.

Also, check your columbine, lenten roses and wallflowers for seedlings that may have come up during the summer. If they are too crowded, transplant seedlings to another location. Columbine can take over an entire area.

Don't forget to water azaleas, rhododendron and camellias. This is a critical time for their newly formed flower buds. Very often azaleas don't bloom in the spring because of improper watering the previous fall.

Late summer to early fall is also the best time to transplant your poppies, which should have begun to peep back through the

soil after resting from their spring performance. Many varieties like a coarse soil. They can be difficult to transplant, but once they find a home, they will cheerfully bloom for decades.

Your lawn may not look as if it's worth it, but "dollar spot" will show up on some turf grasses in the Kentuckiana area in the fall. The disease, which hits in humid days when temperatures are between 70 and 80 degrees, produces bleached spots about the size of silver dollars in your lawn.

If the infection is heavy, the spots can overlap and produce dead areas of turf. There's not much you can do except let the disease run its course, then reseed. But if you feed your lawn high-nitrogen fertilizer twice every fall, as you should, chances are dollar spot won't develop at all.

Remember, it's not too late to start a fall salad garden. Lettuce, spinach, mustard greens, radishes, onions and kale often do better in cool fall weather. Just a few square feet of garden space will give you fresh vegetables into October. Be sure to spray with a fungicide such as Maneb or Zineb; fungus is a real problem in the humid fall weather.

LATE

I remember my grandmother picking gooseberries for gooseberry pie, and with some care you can have them too.

Plant gooseberries in the fall, spacing plants about five feet apart, and setting them two to three inches deeper than they were growing when purchased.

Immediately after planting, cut all canes to six to eight inches above ground level. The first winter after planting, cut all but the six strongest canes back to ground level. Thereafter, prune each winter, cutting out the three oldest canes and all but three of the new season's growth. With this system, each of the plants will bear fruit on one-, two- or three-year-old canes, producing a maximum crop.

Gooseberries need regular fertilizing. In late winter feed a tablespoon of potassium sulfate per square yard. In early spring add a tablespoon of ammonium sulfate per square yard. Every three years add two tablespoons of superphosphate every square yard.

Start picking when the berries are pea-sized and use the larger berries that follow for pies just like Grandma used to bake.

If you grew popcorn this year, you must pick it before the first frosts, which often occur in early October. If you wait too long, frost will cause mold on the ears.

At harvest, the moisture level for most popcorn will be about 16 percent. The best popping moisture is about 13.5 percent. To dry the corn, the husks should be removed and the ears hung to dry in a warm, well-ventilated area. After two to three weeks, toss some kernels into a popper and check to see if all of them pop.

If not, wait a week and try again. The popcorn is ready when all of the kernels pop. There are a lot worse ways of doing research.

Store the kernels in an airtight container. They can last years if kept cool or frozen.

It's not too soon to prepare a garden area — maybe even a raised bed — for next year's pea plantings. Peas can be planted as early as March and preparing the ground now can make it easier. With a small raised bed, you'll be able to cover the area with clear plastic, getting a big jump on the season.

If you want your poinsettias to put out red bracts in time for Christmas, begin placing them in total darkness for 15 hours a day from very late September to early October. Keep them in bright light the other nine hours of the day.

Some people use paper bags pulled well down over the plant; others go as far as putting the plants in a closet. It is important that the darkness be total; even a few hours of light in that 15-hour period can prevent the bracts from co-operating. It usually takes eight to 10 weeks for the bracts to show red. After that, normal care will carry the plants to Christmas.

If you keep the poinsettias in a cool place with indirect light, they will stay healthy for many weeks after Christmas.

FRED'S TIPS

Gardening season may be almost over, but that doesn't mean there's not some pesticides left in their containers in the garage. They can be saved, and here's the best way to do it:

Store them in a locked room or cabinet where children can't get close to them. Don't store them near feed, seed or garden clothing. Store them in well-lighted, ventilated areas that will not freeze. Store them in their original containers and mark the purchase date on the sides of the containers so you'll know their age. Keep an up-to-date inventory.

Although spring is usually the biggest sales period for mail-order nurseries, we still order many plants for the fall season. So here are some tips to help avoiding ordering problems.

To help people determine if a particular tree or plant can survive the local winters, the continental United States is divided into "hardness zones," with northern Wisconsin being a "3" and the southern tip of Florida a "10." Indiana and Kentucky fall into zones 5, 6 and 7. To be

sure your plants will survive even the toughest Kentucky winters, order plants that are hardy in zone 5, which means they should survive temperatures of 20 degrees below zero.

Don't be misled by fantastic claims. Trees that grow 20 feet a year — and that is virtually impossible outside of Brazil — are usually very brittle and susceptible to ice and wind damage.

If you have any doubts about a product, contact your local agriculture agents. They are well-trained people and can save you a lot of money.

When the pumpkins in your garden are full-sized but not fully hardened, let your children and their friends pick out their pumpkins and inscribe their names on them. Use a nail or small screwdriver but don't write too deeply. As the pumpkins mature, the names will harden into the rind.

If you really feel ambitious, you might have them write a poem, a message, or even the Gettysburg Address.

Keep checking your pets for fleas, which are a real problem this time of year. Use flea collars, give them regular baths with flea powder and check the furniture for evidence that the pests have moved inside, often with your pet as the moving service.

Be wary of any advertisements claiming that ultrasonic-sound devices can scare insects from your yard or house. Research done by the U.S. Department of Agriculture show they don't work, especially the ones that are supposed to stop mosquitoes from biting. Stick with repellents, screens and fly swatters.

Not all plant problems stem from improper environment or attacks of pests and diseases. All houseplants eventually die from having lived long, happy lives.

The popular piggyback plant is a case in point. No matter how well you care for it, eventually the time comes when it is spent and must be discarded — but not before you have rooted some of the baby plants that began life on top of the old leaves, hence the name piggyback.

To propagate the piggyback, clip the mature leaf and the accompanying smaller plant, set it on the soil surface, secure with a bobby pin and water. After the plantlet forms its own roots, the old "mother leaf" will wither away.

Tree-stump removal is a problem that haunts many gardeners, especially after a bad spell of summer thunderstorms. There are professionals with big grinding machines that can crunch the stump down below the level of your lawn-mower blade, but they can be very expensive.

You can also buy little cans of "stump decay" products in hardware stores or nurseries, but that can also be expensive. If you've got the time, energy and tools, you can dig out the stumps. An easier solution might be to drill holes in the stump with a large wood bit, then fill the holes with fertilizer. This encourages decay, but it still may be years before the stump disappears.

Contrary to what many people believe, fall fertilizing with slow-release nitrogen can help reduce winter injury to broadleaf and narrow-leafed evergreens and improve spring growth. But — and this is a BIG but — do not apply the fertilizer until after the first killing frost. You do not want to encourage late plant growth.

Protect young, thin-barked trees against frost cracks by wrapping the trunks with protective paper or strips of burlap. Apple, ash, beech, elm, linden, London plane, maple, oak, poplar, tulip tree, walnut and willow are susceptible to cracking.

People often ask me about large, green worms on tomato plants. The worms are bad enough, but what's really strange-looking are those white spiny objects on their backs.

The big worm is the tomato hornworm, and I never use an insecticide on him; he's so big I just pick him off. The white objects are cocoons of a parasitic wasp — the braconid. It lays its eggs on the back of the hornworm and as the young emerge they eat the hornworm. It's not a pleasant thought, but those wasps are just part of the mostly unseen insect world that gets us through a season.

A Purdue entomologist recently warned that yellow-jacket nests can be hazardous to the health of people living nearby, and eradication should only be tried at night when the swarming insects have returned home. There are "long-range" sprays available, but John McDonald advised homeowners to get professional extermination help for any nests found inside buildings.

Cut the heads from your sunflower stalks just as the seeds begin to turn brown and the backs of the heads turn yellow. Hang them upside down in a warm, dry place, like a garage rafter or the attic. Basements are too humid for storage this time of year.

Let the heads hang for about three weeks before removing the seeds. If the seeds start to fall earlier, place paper bags around the heads. Just for the record, the tallest sunflower ever recorded was 17 feet, 3 inches. The widest known head was 33 1/4 inches.

One of the methods I've heard to keep deer out of your pasture, yard or garden is to hang Dial soap around the place. Even if it doesn't work, you'll have clean mosquitoes.

Think about using gourds around the house as fall and winter decorations. If you didn't raise any, you can often find them at farmer's markets. Dry them well and wax or shellack them for more shine.

If your azaleas are looking a little on the pale green side, the problem could be an iron deficiency called chlorosis. To correct the problem, treat the plants with chelated iron or iron sulfate. Spray it directly onto the leaf surface or soak the soil around the plant.

This treatment is also good for young pines and gardenias that look pale green around the gills. It also works on baby pin oaks.

FRED'S SUPER TIP

If your lawn looks like something a weed collector would envy, now is the time to do something about it. Early September is the best time of the year to sow grass seed for a better-looking landscape.

Kentucky is known as the Bluegrass State, but bluegrass is no longer considered the best choice for lawns in Kentucky and Southern Indiana.

True, bluegrass does make a beautiful lawn. But bluegrass is a high-maintenance grass; it is much like growing a rose garden in that it requires a lot of care. Bluegrass needs a lot of water during summer stress; it is also prone to diseases, grub damage and thatch buildup.

So if you are the type who likes to spend your spare time fishing, golfing or going on long trips, I would recommend you try the new tall fescues. Keep in mind that if you do intend to switch grass varieties, it is best to kill out existing grass with a total-kill herbicide like Roundup or Kleenup, as we suggested in August, and start from scratch. It is not a good idea to try to seed fescue into an existing bluegrass lawn.

The main advantages to tall fescue are that it adapts to full sun or medium shade, performs well in heavy clay or sandy soils, tolerates traffic well, has no serious insect problems, is competitive with weeds, doesn't create much buildup, requires little if any irrigation and is faster to establish than Kentucky bluegrass.

However, since nothing in this world is perfect, there are some problems with tall fescue. It requires more frequent mowing than bluegrass, it develops some brown patch disease in hot summers, it isn't very resilient and lateral spread is very slow.

If you want to sow tall fescue, remember to sow it thickly, at least six pounds per 1,000 square feet.

What about perennial ryegrasses? University of Kentucky turf specialist Dr. A.J. Powell says most perennial ryegrasses are not reliable and form a clumpy, open turf that has little appeal and poor persistence.

When seeded alone, ryegrasses may not survive the summer unless irrigation and disease control are provided; although not adapted to heavy shade, they will often survive in such areas and are easily re-established.

The major advantages of rye-

grass are that it has a fine texture similar to bluegrass, is more tolerant than other grasses to heavy clay and compacted soils, germinates quickly (five to seven days), has excellent seedling vigor, has no thatch problem, tolerates traffic well, can be mowed short (about one inch, if desired), will often dominate weeds and can be sown with minimum soil preparation.

Major drawbacks to perennial ryegrass is that it is somewhat difficult to mow (it requires a sharp mower), is susceptible to summer brown patch disease, has little heat tolerance (a major problem in our summer weather), needs summer watering if a thick stand is established and has little resiliency.

Regardless of what kind of grass seed you decide to sow, remember that the seed must come in contact with the soil when it is sown. Spreading the seed on top of an existing stand of grass, especially where there is a layer of thatch between the grass and the soil, is simply a waste of time and money.

That means you must rent a dethatching machine to pull up the accumulated organic matter on top of the soil and leave small slits in the earth for seeds to fall into.

Wait to apply fall nitrogen fertilizer until after the seeds have germinated and don't apply weedkillers until the new grass has been mowed at least twice.

NOTES

OCTOBER

OCTOBER CHECKLIST

EARLY

☐ Harvest green tomatoes before killing frost.
☐ Fall plow garden.
☐ Harvest sweet potatoes.
☐ Bring in all houseplants before temperatures drop below 55 degrees; check for insects and water less; do not repot.
☐ Keep weeds out of the garden.
☐ Sow grass seed and fertilize at the same time.
☐ Bring pots of gerbera daisies indoors.
☐ Plant a cover crop of rye or barley over the garden.
☐ Prepare Christmas cactuses for blooming.
☐ Fertilize lawn.
☐ Plant trees.

MIDDLE

☐ Move those perennials.
☐ Harvest winter squash.
☐ Plant full-grown mums.
☐ Harvest horseradish roots.
☐ Wrap trunks of young, deciduous trees.
☐ Protect evergreens, azaleas and rhododendrons from drying winter winds.

LATE

☐ Plant spring-flowering bulbs to be forced indoors early next season.
☐ Prune trees.
☐ Clean and store tools, lawn mower and tiller.

SUPER TIP

☐ Planting the bulb garden.

October is for poets, fans of Indian summer and little children who want to parade around the neighborhood looking like ghosts, goblins and fairy princesses.

The leaves change into great bursts of crimson, russet and gold, the garden chores are almost finished, and it's time to sit on the back porch and reflect that another year has almost past — and it's so good to be a part of it.

October comes from the Latin word for "eight"; its location as the 10th month of the year is the work of the Romans. The average high temperature in the Louisville area is a crisp 69.2 degrees; the average low 46.2 degrees. The average October rainfall is 2.63 inches.

The wettest October in history was in 1883, when 8.05 inches fell. The driest October was in 1907, when only .07 inches of rain fell, the driest month in local history.

The highest recorded temperature for the month was 92 degrees, which occurred Oct. 2, 1953, and Oct. 4 and 5, 1959. The all-time low was 23 degrees, set on Oct. 29, 1925, and Oct. 23, 1952.

The earliest snowfall in local history occurred on Oct. 3, 1980, when a trace fell across Kentuckiana. The heaviest October snowfall was the 1.2 inches that fell on Oct. 23, 1937.

By the way, the average annual snowfall for the Louisville area is about 18 inches.

There are 11 hours and 48 minutes of sun on Oct. 1, and 10 hours and 37 minutes on Oct. 31. The average soil temperature varies from 53 to 62 degrees.

Columbus landed in America on Oct. 12, 1492, and slightly over 400 years later, on Oct. 1, 1896, free rural mail delivery began in the United States. The price has gone up considerably since.

EARLY

We're starting to get near the time when frost will zap your tomato plants. If the weatherman calls for a frost, you can save a lot of those green tomatoes by picking them and bringing them indoors to ripen.

The easiest way is to pull up several whole vines and hang them in a dry storage area or shed. I wouldn't bring them indoors to the basement because many tomatoes are infected with whiteflies this time of year.

I prefer to pick tomatoes that are mature and green or just beginning to change color. We use the smaller ones for pickling.

Keep the ripest tomatoes at room temperature, and they should ripen in a week. Mature green tomatoes should be spread out in a single layer OUT OF DIRECT LIGHT. At 60 to 70 degrees they'll ripen in two weeks. Wrapping each tomato in old newspaper or the pages of an old phone book keeps them in good condition.

Another way to ripen tomatoes indoors came from a friend who is not an expert in gardening but in sports — Cawood Ledford. He said he had good luck putting green tomatoes in a Styrofoam cooler along with an apple or two. The apples give off ethylene gas, which promotes ripening.

If you can, try plowing the garden now to get it ready for next year. It will get you off to a quicker start next spring, will allow the ground to warm up faster and will help the compost or leaves you add to the soil rot more efficiently.

It's about time to harvest your sweet potatoes. They are best harvested when the vines begin to yellow. Even a light frost will kill the vines, and soil temperatures below 50 degrees will damage the tuber.

After digging the potatoes, leave them exposed for two to three hours to dry thoroughly, then move them to a warm, humid room or area for two weeks to totally cure.

These conditions are hard to produce, but I had good luck storing them in a black plastic bag in front of a sunny window in the attic of the garage and even in the basement. Sweet potatoes actually improve during storage because part of their starch content turns to sugar.

Every October I get calls from people about houseplants loosing their leaves after they've been brought back indoors for the winter. In every case the gardener waited too long to bring the plant inside, although a change in the amount of light a plant gets will also cause some leaf drop.

In any event, bring them in before nighttime temperatures drop to 55 degrees.

And don't bring the insects indoors with the plants. If the plant is small, tie a plastic bag around the pot and stem and wash the leaves in soapy water. For larger plants use a garden hose, or insecticide, being sure to get under the leaves.

You don't want to repot the indoor plants that have been outside all summer, even if they have long roots coming out of their drainage holes. Repotting will only encourage growth at a time when the plants need to take a break. Just take a sharp knife and cut off the roots. And remember, don't use fertilizer during the fall and winter. That also encourages growth.

Water less — only when the top inch of soil feels dry or if the foliage begins to droop. Never let the plants sit in water. It encourages root rot.

As hard as it can be to maintain your gardening enthusiasm this time of year, it's important to keep your garden as weed-free as possible. Many of the most noxious weeds go to seed this time of year, and if you deal with them now, you won't have to deal with their children and grandchildren next year.

If you're totally desperate and behind in your chores, run the lawn mower over the garden plot to keep the weeds from forming seed heads, and then till the ground.

For those of you still trying to repair the damage to your lawn caused by disease or the late invasion of white grubs, let me give you this hint: We are late in the season for sowing seed, but it can be done if the weather stays warm and there is moisture.

If you're sowing grass seed now, I'd fertilize at the same time. The fertilizer, in light application, will create additional heat as it activates. Water the lawn at least twice a day.

If you're trying to start seeds in a small area, cover the area with burlap and keep it damp. Seeds beneath the burlap should germinate in five to seven days. Just remember to remove the burlap as soon as the seeds sprout.

Big, proud gerbera daisies have become very popular in recent years, but they will not survive outdoors all winter. Since the daisies are traditionally raised in pots, just bring the pots indoors and keep them near bright sun; also, keep the soil moist and warm. Otherwise they may go dormant and die back to the soil. You want to keep them rested but not comatose. Next spring just plant the whole pot in the ground. They're easier to care for that way.

Here's a reminder: A cover crop of rye or barley sown over the garden can be very beneficial if you haven't been able to plow this fall. When it is plowed under next spring it will add organic matter to the soil and will protect the ground from erosion all winter. The seeds for such crops can be broadcast by hand.

Another reminder that if you want your Thanksgiving and Christmas cactuses to bloom for the holidays, they need bright sun during the day and COMPLETE darkness at night. Light, even from a street light, will throw the plants off schedule. It's also important to withhold water from the cactuses. Don't let them get bone-dry, but keep them on the dry side.

Once the buds have formed, gradually resume normal watering and bring them into a bright room where you can enjoy them all day.

Fall, not spring, is the very best time to fertilize lawns. Applications of high-nitrogen fertilizers such as 27-3-3 in October, November and even December — weather permitting — will extend the green color in the fall, provide earlier green in the spring, increase turf intensity and eliminate weeds. Fertilize your lawn NOW.

October — and even November — is also an excellent time to plant trees. Most woody plants need less water in the fall to survive, and even if a tree is without leaves its roots will continue to grow as long as the soil is moist and the ground temperature is above 40 degrees. The roots can get a better, ah, foothold, without competition from the leaves. Then, in the spring, the leaves can take advantage of a strong root system. It's one big, happy partnership.

MIDDLE

Cruise around all parts of your perennial garden and look for lilies, irises, peonies and others that can be moved while there is still some sunshine. It's getting very late. They can be moved now if you must, but this should have been done in July.

If you've been waiting to harvest your winter squash, the ol' calendar on the wall says it's time to get moving. Acorn, spaghetti and butternut squash are ready when the fruit turns a deeper, solid color and the rind is hard.

Butternut squash will turn from greenish-yellow to solid tan, spaghetti squash changes from light to bright yellow, and acorn squash adds a bronze or orange glow on a dark-green background. Leave a two-inch hunk of the stem on the squash to protect the fruit from rot.

If you're tired of a dull, dreary flower garden, a garden that was done in by hot, dry weather, you can brighten the scene considerable by planting full-grown mums now.

Mums — or chrysanthemums for long — are one flower you can transplant when in full bloom. They should be planted before hard winter weather to give them a chance to get established. The U.S. Department of Agriculture suggests you prepare

a soil bed about 10 days before you plant. Dig and loosen the soil to a depth of six inches. Just before planting, respade the soil bed to kill weeds seeds that have germinated.

As you plant the mums — and there are dozens of colors and varieties, so plan carefully — press the soil firmly to eliminate air pockets. Space them from two to 2 1/2 feet apart in well-drained soil. Water well, and you could have color into November.

After the hard frost does hit, cut the tops to ground level and mulch, which will protect them against winter freezing and thawing. When they begin growing again next year, pinch them back several times to force them to spread.

If you're growing horseradish — the perfect Derby Day condiment — remember that it makes its greatest growth in late summer and autumn. For that reason, harvesting the roots is best done just before the ground freezes.

Remember to cut off "sets" of roots eight to 14 inches long to refrigerate over the winter. In the spring you can begin next season's crop.

Here's another reminder to wrap all your young, deciduous trees with long strips of burlap or sisal paper to prevent sunscald and frost damage. Such damage occurs during warms days and freezing nights. This weakens the tree, and a severe winter or dry spell the next summer can kill it.

Evergreens, including azaleas and rhododendrons, are very susceptible to drying winter winds. If you have a small clump, you can protect it behind a burlap screen — burlap stapled to four stakes driven into the ground. Or you can buy a can of anti-desiccant spray. The spray coats the plant with latex, allowing it to breathe but not lose moisture. Use it just before serious cold weather sets in.

LATE

It's not too late to plant some bulbs in pots so you can force them to bloom indoors early next spring. Place choice bulbs in a pot with their tips above the soil, moisten the soil and refrigerate for 10 to 13 weeks. Then move to a cool, bright room and water.

Fall and early winter are good times to prune your trees. It is a very tricky process that must be done correctly or you can seriously damage the tree.

If you're just doing some trimming, be sure your pruning cuts are made flush with the tree. If you leave stubs, they may rot, which could damage the trunk and inner tissue.

In general, you should remove dead limbs, limbs that rub together and narrow, V-shaped crotches.

If you're putting away your tools for the winter, clean off all the mud. Wipes the blades of the clippers and pruners and apply a few drops of oil to all moving parts. Dig out all the booklets and warranty information that came with your mower and tiller to find out how to properly store them for the winter.

FRED'S TIPS

Any nuts that happen to be growing on trees around your house should be allowed to mature fully on the tree and then fall naturally, or with some mild shaking. Gather them daily and allow them to air-dry. Store them in a cool, dry area.

Heavy rains often bring a crop of mushrooms popping up through the ground, usually in places where old lumber, logs or tree roots are buried. They will not damage the lawn and will disappear in colder, drier weather. If you can't wait, just mow them down or rake them up.

If you're planting ground cover in the fall, be sure to put down a two-inch layer of mulch to protect the baby plants. Otherwise freezing and thawing can heave them out of the ground.

If you're thinking of planting some trees this fall, you're better off avoiding magnolia, dogwood, sweet gum and yellowwood. They are unusually susceptible to winter damage and are better planted in the spring.

If trees and shrubs are newly planted, you should withhold fertilizer for a year to allow the plant to get well-established in its new home. Then you can give it a growing boost.

Octobers go much easier if you have a handy stack of cloth, plastic sheets, newspapers, cardboard boxes, wooden boxes or old drapes to serve as protection against frost. Often there will be a hard freeze followed by several more weeks of warm Indian summer, and if you protect your flowers, you can keep the colors alive for a long time.

As tough as it can be to do, now is a good time to take a good look at the trees in your yard to determine if they are growing too close together. We all hate to remove trees, especially those we've nursed from babies, but if you weed them out, the survivors will be stronger, healthier and will probably fill in the gap left by the missing tree. So be fair, but be firm. You're better off in the long run.

Here's a tip that could raise a stink even if it works. Henry Converse, a member of the Kentucky Nut Growers Association, reported that squirrels can be repelled by emptying the contents of cat-litter boxes around the bases of nut trees. The litter can even be placed in perforated bags and hung from the trees, but it must be replaced as the odor fades or dries out. If you have a lot of nut trees, however, you'll need a lot of cats.

Onions can be easily stored by braiding the tops together and hanging them in the kitchen for easy access. They may create a "tearful" odor for a time, but the onions will also be very handy.

If you're looking way down the road and want to plant trees that will produce a wide variety of fall colors, here are a few trees and their autumn colors: red maple, intense red; sugar maple, orange and yellow; sumac, deep scarlet; black gum and ash, deep wine; red oak, dull red; white oak, hazy brown; hickory, light gold; elm, lemon.

If you want to avoid bringing a lot of bugs into your house along with the firewood, you can minimize the problem by taking a few precautions. Don't stack the wood against the house or another building; it keeps the bugs dry and warm. Bring in only the wood you can burn in a few days. Do not leave firewood in the house over the summer. Don't bother with insecticides; it's unnecessary and expensive and could be hazardous to your health when you burn the wood.

All those leaves falling from your trees can greatly improve your garden soil, especially heavy clay and sandy soils. If possible — and just running over them with the lawn mower will help — shred the leaves before spreading them over the garden. Then till them in. You'll be amazed at how your soil will improve in a few years.

FRED'S SUPER TIP

Home gardeners are coming out of nurseries these days with armloads of bags filled with bulbs. Mention bulbs and most people think of tulips, hyacinths and narcissus. But the truth is flowering bulbs come in an almost unending array and produce blooms of various sizes and colors.

With careful planning, your spring bulb garden can have bright splashes of color beginning with the yellow winter aconite in February or March and lasting through the final late-blooming tulip in May.

Planning on paper is an easy way to redecorate your garden. Bulbs require little garden space and can be planted in annual and perennial flower beds, among shrubs, under trees and in almost every part of the landscape.

Begin your bulb plan by making a scale drawing of your garden area. Roughly draw in where you would like bulbs to be planted. Check the growing conditions of the area. Remember, the most important element in growing bulbs in our clay-type soil is GOOD DRAINAGE. Dig a hole about six inches deep and fill it with water. If the water is still there an hour later, choose another location. When planting, check the depth chart that comes with the package. A general rule of thumb is to plant the bulb about three times deeper than its own length, and, please, please, pointed side up.

If the soil is very hard and dry, use an auger the diameter of your bulbs. Attach it to your electric drill, and wrap a piece of white tape around the auger at the depth you want plant the bulb. It's a heckuva lot faster and easier on the wrist than using a hand-planter.

Plant snowdrops, anemone and crocus for borders, grape hyacinth, oxalis and scilla for four- to eight-inch tall blooms and tulips, narcissus and hyacinths as background plantings.

Spring-flowering bulbs should be planted in October to insure good root development before winter. The better the root system, the better the flowers will be in the spring. Buy early and be sure to select large, firm, plump bulbs or roots. Do not purchase any that are bruised, blemished or soft.

If you do not get a chance to plant them in October, don't fret. I have planted tulips as late as January. That was not by choice, however, I forgot where I put them in the storage shed.

As further proof that late fall planting works, have you ever enjoyed the tulip gardens at Churchill Downs during Derby Week? Donnie Lord, the Downs chief gardener, does all of his spring tulip planting after the fall racing meet is over and that is usually after Thanksgiving.

If you don't get them in the ground, toss them out. They will never survive a full year out of the ground.

When you dig the hole for the spring bulbs, put a little bone meal in the bottom of the hole for good root development. But remember, the most important time to feed bulbs is in the spring, just as the new growth is beginning to develop from the ground.

Are you a patio gardener? You can enjoy tulips next spring if you plant bulbs this fall in boxes or other containers that are at least a foot deep and have drainage holes. I know one gardener who has had spring bulbs in planters around his condominium every year for the last six years, regardless of how cold the winters get.

If squirrels frequent your yard, put pieces of chicken wire over your tulip plantings. The mesh should be fine enough to keep the pests from digging up the bulbs but coarse enough to let the stems of the bulbs emerge in the spring.

NOTES

NOVEMBER

NOVEMBER CHECKLIST

EARLY

☐ Remove leaves and any weak stems from bottoms of roses.
☐ Plant deciduous trees; stake for support.
☐ Sketch out what you'd like to plant next year; clean up the garden; fall plow.
☐ Remove leaves from lawn.
☐ Consider building a compost heap.
☐ Move houseplants closer to sunny windows; water less frequently and withhold fertilizer.
☐ Force bulbs indoors for spring blooming.
☐ Continue preparing poinsettias to put out red bracts.
☐ Put screens around smaller trees to keep rabbits and mice away.
☐ Dig the hole for living Christmas tree.
☐ Fertilize lawn.
☐ Complete harvest and storage of root crops.
☐ Collect seeds from flowers and store.
☐ Transplant scented geraniums, creeping rosemary, lemon verbena and bay and move indoors.

MIDDLE

☐ Continue to water evergreens; tie up branches to avoid damage from heavy accumulations of ice and snow.
☐ Drain and cover bird baths; stock bird feeders.
☐ Stock up on gardening materials for next season.
☐ Continue to plant hardy bulbs; take in tubers and corms from dahlias, caladiums, cannas and gladioluses.
☐ Cut mums back to ground level.
☐ Fertilize trees after first killing frost.
☐ Finish harvesting gourds.

LATE

☐ Cut roses back, spray with miticide and fungicide and mulch.
☐ Mulch strawberry plants.
☐ Remove any remaining fruit from fruit trees and clean area underneath to discourage rodents.
☐ Clean and store lawn mower.

SUPER TIP

☐ Safely burning firewood.

Ah, November, with its cheerful fires, Thanksgiving celebrations and, if you're lucky, time for just one more walk in the woods before the snow flies.

November is the month when the bright colors give way to yellows and grays, and winter's frozen breath creeps under the doors and past windows. But it's also the height of football season, and can basketball be far behind?

November takes its name from **novem,** the Latin word for nine. Because July was named for Julius Caesar and August for Augustus Caesar, the Roman senate did offer to name November after Tiberius Caesar. He declined, saying, "What would you do if there are 13 emperors?"

The average high temperature in November is 55.5 degrees; the average low 36.6 degrees. The average precipitation — melted snow included — is 3.49 inches.

The most precipitation ever in November is the 9.12 inches that fell in 1957; the least was the .25 inches in 1904. The highest recorded temperature in November was 84 degrees on Nov. 17, 1958. The coldest day was minus 1 degree on Nov. 25, 1950.

The average first date for snowfall in our area is Nov. 16, although it can fall well before — or after — that. The normal snowfall for the month is 1.5 inches, but 13.2 inches fell in November 1966, including 13 inches on one day, Nov. 3, in Louisville. The odd thing was the temperature never dropped below 34 degrees, and the snow was extremely heavy and wet, killing thousands of birds at a nearby poultry farm.

There are 10 hours and 35 minutes of sun on Nov. 1 and nine hours and 45 minutes on Nov. 30. The average soil temperature ranges between 50 and 54 degrees.

The first intercollegiate football game in the United States was played on Nov. 6, 1869, between Rutgers and Princeton, and Saturday and Sunday meals in this country have been eaten in front of television sets ever since.

EARLY

Just because it's early November doesn't mean it's time to send roses "beddy-bye" for the year. Don't get in a big hurry to cut them back and winterize them. Most rose growers I know like to have two or three nights when temperatures drop into the low 20s before they begin the process.

You need several cold nights to harden the stems and slow down the upward movement of water. That should occur in a few weeks.

Is there anything you can do in the meantime? Sure. Put on a pair of gloves and strip off the leaves to about 15 inches above ground. Then take a good look at the plant. If you see any small, weak, spindly stems, remove them. Leave five good, strong stems on each plant.

Most years, early November remains a good time to plant deciduous plants because even if their tops are dormant, the root system can continue to grow and become well-established. However, I would plant only balled and burlapped or container-grown plants; bare-root planting is very tricky this time of year.

In checking trees for purchase, be sure the branch tips have healthy buds with just a little sign of green. Check the ends of some branches by lightly nicking them with your fingernail. A live branch will show a little green. Please be careful; if 100 people check the same tree it could be killed by "Fingernail Fungus."

Large trees should be supported with stakes driven into the soil outside the planting hole. One trick is to save your old garden hose, then cut it into small sections and thread the support string through it.

Bend the hose around the tree; this will keep the string from cutting into the bark. Wrap the trees in special tree wrap to protect them from the freeze-thaw cycle.

November is a good time to look over the past growing season and plan next year's activities. Draw a sketch of what you have and what you plan to add. Makes notes on what worked and what didn't; there's room at the back of every chapter in this book to do just that.

Give your planning some thought. Look ahead a few years. A tiny tree planted now could be eating your eaves in 10 years. The gardening pace has slowed now and you have time to think and to scan the catalogs.

Don't forget to clean up your garden, fall-plow it if possible and have your soil tested to see what nutrients you'll need for next year. It's so important you do that.

Don't leave a carpet of leaves on your lawn. It's the best way I know to kill the grass. Rake or pick up those leaves. A lawn mower with a bagger attached can save a lot of aching muscles and liniment later. Think about starting a compost bin so you can improve your soil later this fall or early next spring.

It's easy. One simple way is to just pound four stakes in the ground for corners, and wrap hardware cloth about three feet tall around them. Build your compost pile near the garden. Dump in shredded leaves and grass clippings until they are about six to 10 inches deep. Then sprinkle 1 1/2 cups of 10-10-10 fertilizer and 2/3 cup of dolomitic limestone. Keep adding layers of leaves, clippings, garbage scraps and fertilizer. You'll be amazed at how quickly the compost will "work" if you keep the pile moist and keep turning it over with a rake or shovel. It will make the perfect garden additive.

As houseplant growth slows, apply less and less fertilizer and water. You might move the plants closer to sunnier windows if they are dropping too many leaves, although that's normal for many plants this time of year.

It's not too late to "force" bulbs indoors for early spring. Pot a few with the tips of the bulbs just above the soil line, moisten the soil and refrigerate for 10 to 13 weeks. Then transfer to a cool, sunny location and allow three to four weeks for the indoor blooms.

Continue keeping your poinsettias in complete darkness for 14 to 15 hours. But please, please remember to put them in bright light the rest of the time. I can't tell you how many times people have left their plants in the closet 24 hours a day, then wondered why they died.
Continue the process until the red bracts begin to show, then put them in cool, bright light. If you keep them in a cool room, they'll bloom for weeks after Christmas.

Tour the yard. Be sure to place metal screens around the smaller trees to keep the rabbits and mice from gnawing at the bark. Sometimes you can buy enough old screens at a yard sale to provide tree protection for years. Hardware cloth works well too.
Keep the screen a few inches away from the trunk and push it a few inches into the ground to keep the burrowing rodents away. A short rod or stick will help. If you don't use screening, at least pull all the mulch a few inches away from the tree so the rodents won't spend the winter living next to it.

If you're planning to order a live Christmas tree, it will help to dig the hole now while the digging is good. Put the dirt in buckets or baskets and store it in the garage or basement.

Late fall fertilizing remains important. Grass roots can remain active in temperatures as low as 35 to 40 degrees. Apply two to four pounds of high-nitrogen fertilizer in a water-soluble form, per 1,000 square feet of lawn. The bad news is you should keep mowing the lawn until growth stops.

Finish harvesting your root crops and store them in a cool, humid location. If humidity is a problem, store them in perforated plastic bags, which will help.

If you feel adventurous, you might try collecting seeds from some of your favorite flowers and store them in small, airtight containers at a temperature of 35 to 55 degrees.
Be warned: If you collect hybrid seeds, the flowers you grow next year may not be exactly the same as those you planted; hybrid seeds will revert to one of their ancestors.
That may not matter. I know of marigolds that came up "volunteer" year after year in the same spot with no appreciable change in color or tenacity. It's always fun to keep a little of last summer for next summer.

Scented geraniums, creeping rosemary, lemon verbena and bay are not hardy in this area, so transplant them into pots so they can be moved indoors, or into a cold frame.

MIDDLE

Soak all the soil around your newer plantings, especially evergreens, to help them through the winter. Use an anti-desiccant spray on especially vulnerable rhododendrons and azaleas. You can even tie up the branches of pyramidal arborvitae and other upright evergreens with heavy twine to avoid possible damage from heavy ice and snow accumulations, although such storms do not occur in this area every winter.

Drain and cover bird baths and shallow garden pools to avoid winter damage and get to work buying or repairing the bird feeders; the birds will need some winter feed soon enough. Your local Audubon Society chapter often sponsors autumn bird-seed sales, with the profits going to help the organization, so watch for a sale.

If you do a lot of outdoor gardening — or indoor for that matter — this is the season to stock up on planting soil, fertilizer, pre-emergents, mulch and peat moss at bargain rates. Be sure to check bags for damage and spills.

You can continue to plant tulips, daffodils, crocus, lilies and other hardy bulbs as long as you can work the ground, or at least until Thanksgiving. Well-drained soil is essential for good bulbs. Most prefer partial shade. Mass them in large groupings for better effect.

If you haven't taken in the dahlia, caladium, canna and gladiolus tubers for winter storage, you're asking for trouble. All are vulnerable to heavy frost. Store them in a cool, dry place. Check monthly and throw out the rotten ones.

Cut mums back to ground level after they are finished blooming and cover with a light mulch after the first hard freeze.

Fertilize your trees with a high-nitrogen fertilizer AFTER the first hard killing frost; applying fertilizer too soon will promote growth that could be killed by the winter cold. The general recommendation is three pounds of actual nitrogen per 1,000 square feet of root area. Fertilize at least twice the distance from the trunk to the drip line to ensure that all feeder roots get some nourishment.

Finish harvesting your gourds. Wash them well, let them dry for four weeks and protect them with wax or even clear shellac.

Don't neglect your lawn mower. After disconnecting the spark plug — you DO want to be a 10-fingered gardener next year — break loose the caked material from the blade and inside the housing. Clean the whole mower with soap and water. Run the engine briefly, drain the oil, replace it with new oil and run a few more minutes. Be sure to reattach the spark plug before that, or you may get a little frustrated.

Then drain all the gas, running the engine until it's all gone. Remove the plug, pour a tablespoon of oil into the hole, turn the blade a few revolutions by hand to coat the inside of the engine, then replace the plug. Clean the air filter. Sharpen the blade. Park the lawn mower inside. Don't think about grass for four months.

LATE

OK, it should be about time to put those roses to bed for the winter. The late Charlie Dawson, a good friend and one of Kentucky's foremost rose growers, always recommended a final spraying of miticide to kill red spider mites as part of the final chores.

So cut the roses back to about 12 to 14 inches, remove any remaining foliage, spray them with a mix of miticide and fungicide. You should never mix anything with a miticide during the growing season, but in the dormant season it's fine.

You can mulch with any good shredded or chunk bark mulch, or you can use garden dirt. Be sure the soil is from another part of the garden so you don't dig around the roses and injure the roots.

If you are prepared and brought in some soil last month to stash between the roses, you can get a jump on the project. Plus you'll have some mulch material handy in the event of a cold snap.

Whatever material you use, mound it over the base of the plant at least eight to 10 inches high. It will settle, and you may have to add more mulch later. In a really cold winter, you might heap it over the stubs.

Be sure not to mulch too early.

Wait until the ground has a crust to it. The mulch isn't to keep the plants warm over the winter. It's to keep the ground at a fairly cold temperature so the plants don't heave out in the winter months.

Climbing roses also need protection when winter temperatures drop near zero. When such weather is near, lay the canes on the ground, hold them down with pins or notched stakes and cover them with several inches of mulch stored in the garage.

If you have tree roses, wrap the heads of the plants in straw and cover with burlap. If sub-zero weather is on the way, dig carefully under the roots on one side of the plants — it may take a jackhammer — and pull the plants over, being careful not to break the root connectors. Then cover them with soil and straw. Come spring, set the plants upright again. It makes it easier for the Japanese beetles to find them.

It's also time to prepare your strawberries for a long winter's nap. Strawberries have shallow root systems, which are very susceptible to breaking when the ground freezes. Plan to apply a mulch to strawberries after growth has slowed, often following a week of temperatures in the 40s in the day and in the 20s at night but before the thermometer hits the single-digit numbers.

You should mulch strawberries with clean wheat straw. One year while mulching our strawberries, I ran out of straw, got too lazy to go to town for more and used some old, broken hay bales a neighbor offered me. I lived to regret it. The next year I had more weeds than strawberries and ended up plowing under the whole row.

Use about a bale of straw for each 50 feet of strawberry row and fluff it about three inches deep. Next spring, remove the mulch before the berries set out buds so you don't break off the crowns while removing it. Pile the straw between rows because it might be needed again in a cold snap.

You can also help your young fruit trees through the winter by harvesting any fruit that remains and cleaning an area of grass about two feet around the trunk to discourage rodents. Some orchard growers I know also put pea-size gravel around the trunk about 4 to 6 inches wide and deep. It discourages rodents and gives the trees more stability over the winter. Don't do any pruning of grapes or fruit trees now. Wait until the end of February or the first of March.

FRED'S TIPS

While tramping through the woods this fall, you're likely to see a small tree that might look good in your yard. Some of these trees can be moved — AFTER you get permission — but there are tricks to it.

First, be prepared to make two trips to the woods over a two-year period; the first trip to prune the roots, the second to come back a year later and do the moving.

To prune the roots, measure the diameter of the trunk, move out from it one foot for each inch of diameter, then dig a circular trench as deep as your spade can penetrate.

Refill the trench with topsoil, and the tree will form a dense mat of fibrous roots in that new dirt.

The second year — and be sure to move it in early spring or after a hard frost in the fall — you can dig up the tree and take it home. Water well and keep watering.

Very small trees can be moved immediately after a hard frost without digging a trench, but a tree of any size should be moved over a two-year period.

Be careful about changing a tree's habitat. It a tree has been living in the deep shade of the woods, it might die in an open spot in your lawn. It will, at the very least, take years to get going.

Houseplants often suffer from dry indoor air during the winter months, wilting and turning brown at the edges. You can help by humidifying the air around them or placing a tray of wet pebbles below them. Be sure the water in the pebble tray is well below the pot so it doesn't "wick" up into the pot.

Plants grown in containers are less cold-hardy than those grown in the garden because their roots are more exposed to freezing temperatures. You can insulate the roots by burying the pots in the ground or under a pile of sawdust, compost or mulch.

Many people will hastily put their spring bulbs in the ground in the fall, then forget where they put them. Make a chart of what you planted and where. More important, mark the locations with plastic sticks available at all gardening centers. Be sure to use an indelible pen listing the color and height of the plant and the date you put the bulb in the ground. It will prevent your bulbs from becoming lost children next spring.

Wild grape vines are best killed by cutting them off at ground level in late fall and applying a herbicide like Kleenup or Roundup to the green foliage in the spring. A repeat application might be needed later. Be careful not to get the chemical on other plants because it will kill them too.

To help protect your garden tools for next year, sharpen your spades, hoes, shovels and lawn tools and cover them with a light coat of oil. Then they'll be ready to go in the spring.

If you're not sure how to dispose of your empty pesticide containers, the Division of Waste Management of the Kentucky Department for Environmental Protection recommends that you rinse the container three times, drain the rinse water into your sprayer tank for use, then wrap the container in a newspaper and put in the garbage. Plastic and metal containers should be punctured to be sure they are not used again.

We've talked a lot about mulching, but there's also a danger of over-mulching and suffocating the roots over a three- to five-year period. Outside of your roses, keep mulch only a few inches deep around your plants. That will be enough.

Root crops such as carrots, turnips and parsnips can be stored right where they grew in the garden. Cover them with a layer of straw, mulch, leaves or sawdust. It also makes them easier to dig in the winter.

Beets, cabbage, cauliflower, kale, leeks and onions can be stored for several weeks under mulch, but they probably won't last through the winter.

You can also bury a 20-gallon trash container up to its lid in the garden, then pile straw or leaves over the top. It makes a nice root cellar for crop storage. Metal containers are more rodent proof.

Spinach, although not a root crop, is so tough you can bury it under five inches of straw and harvest it all winter. In March, remove the straw and side-dress with ammonium nitrate, and the plants will put out new leaves way ahead of everyone else's.

Herbs such as thyme, parsley, dill, chives, mint and oregano can be grown indoors over the winter in a sunny window. Arti-

ficial light will work if you don't
have a handy window. Pot some
up and try it. Thyme, parsley
and dill can be started from seed.
You'll need cuttings for the others.

You can move your "magic lilies" any time after they have finished blooming and the flowers
have faded. But don't put them
in too much shade, which will
inhibit their growth. It may take
them a year or two after transplanting to fully bloom again.

Because most trees having a
ropelike mesh of roots crisscross-
ing one another, you are often
fertilizing many different trees
when fertilizing the lawn. That's
because most feeder roots grow
within an inch of the surface.
Keep that in mind when fertilizing and when contemplating con-
struction projects. You never
want to put a thick layer of new
dirt beneath a healthy tree; it
could kill it.

The old method of boring
holes to fertilize trees isn't necessary. Granular or liquid fertilizer
spread over the surface will do
the trick.

Remember never to "top" your
tree while pruning it. A lot of
allegedly professional tree people
will recommend it, but such topping throws off the balance between roots and tops, starving
the root system. Topping also
stimulates "rank" growth, which
is soft and weak and opens the
tree to disease.

If you bring a shrub or small
tree home from the nursery and

notice that it's pot-bound — the
roots are massed and circling
thickly around the inside of the
pot or hanging out the bottom —
there's still a way to plant it.

Take the shrub out of its container, use a sharp spade or shovel to cut through the rootball
from 1/3 to 1/2 way up from
the bottom, and then literally
pull the remaining roots apart,
forming an opening.

When planting, press the rootball into the bottom of the hole,
fill around the roots and water.
Trimming the roots and opening
the bottom will encourage the
growth of pot-bound plants.

Buying the biggest tree in the
nursery isn't always the best
idea. Small and medium-sized
trees often begin growing in your
yard more quickly because
they've lost fewer roots in the
transplanting process. Keep that
in mind when buying.

You can save a lot of money
and have a little fun by propagat-
ing forsythia, pussy willow, spirea and quince this fall. Take
10- to 12-inch cuttings after the
plants have dropped their leaves,
dip the cut ends into rooting
hormone and plant them eight to
nine inches deep in a trench.
Keep the trench moist. When the
plants bud out in the spring,
transplant them into containers.
Keep them there for one season
unless they look big enough to
plant the following fall.

When you're thinking about
planting trees this fall, the University of Kentucky recommends
avoiding those that are short-
lived, have weak branches that

make them prone to storm damage, or develop fruit that's more of a nuisance than a treat.

For those reasons, avoid, if possible, box elder, tree of heaven, Lombardy poplar, osage orange, mulberry, silver or water maple, cottonwood, black locust, Siberian elm, European white birch, catalpa and willows.

FRED'S SUPER TIP

With winter banging loudly at the door, let's talk a little bit about chimneys, wood-burning stoves and collecting firewood, a chore millions of Americans are tackling each year.

Improperly maintained chimneys cause 40,000 fires in the United States each year, costing homeowners about $25 million and causing insurance companies to take a much closer look a wood-heated homes and the applicable insurance rates.

Many of those fires are caused by the creosote deposits found in most chimneys. Chimneys should be inspected every year and professionally cleaned to avoid buildup. If you have a wood-burning stove, it won't hurt to inspect and clean it several times a year during warm winter spells.

But you'll still get a creosote buildup just burning wood in an open fireplace, so here are a few tips to keep your fire burning safely, most of them supplied by safety experts from the University of Kentucky:

Flue temperatures must be more than 250 degrees to reduce creosote formation. If the stovepipe is too long or the chamber inside the chimney too big and not designed for wood-burning stoves, creosote will build up. Too many turns in the pipe will also lead to creosote accumulations.

Many experts are recommending that special insulated stovepipes be run from the wood-burning stove or insert up the inside of the chimney, especially in older houses, to prevent creosote buildup.

These are all factors to be considered before purchasing a wood-burning stove or fireplace insert. To be absolutely sure, check with your local fire department or your insurance agent for proper installation techniques.

Burn dry wood, either pine or hardwood that has been cut, split and stacked for at least six months — a year is better. That's because about half the weight of fresh-cut wood is water, which must be evaporated as steam when the wood starts burning. This costs you heat and causes the cooler smoke to condense on the flue as creosote.

In general, softwoods such as pine, soft maple or sycamore will produce more creosote than hardwoods such as ash, beech, oak, hard maple, hickory and locust, but unseasoned wood is the biggest culprit in creosote buildup.

Be sure to deal with reputable wood salesmen. Know exactly what kind of wood you're buying and how long it has been seasoned. Well-seasoned wood is normally a darker color, and the ends have little splits indicating its dryness.

Avoid prolonged periods of burning with the damper turned way down. Slow-burning fires —

and many wood burners will turn their dampers way down at night before going to bed — produce more creosote.

If you insist on that practice, try to compensate by having a hot, vigorous fire for 10 to 15 minutes in the morning to help burn off deposits. It's also smart to start a vigorous fire at night before turning down the damper.

By mixing softwoods with hardwoods you can have an easily ignited but longer-lasting fire. Don't ever burn treated lumber or even lumber scraps you think may have been treated 10 years ago. The preservatives in treated lumber produce very poisonous ashes when burned.

Tests have indicated many of those chemicals sold to put on the fire and prevent creosote buildup are not especially effective and can even produce noxious gases. Use accordingly.

Should a chimney fire occur — and the frightening roar in your chimney will be unmistakable — call the fire department first, and, if possible, cut off the air to the fire by turning down the stove dampers.

Always have a fire extinguisher on hand and be sure there are smoke alarms in every room near the fireplace. A creosote fire can reach 3,000 degrees, and you can't be too careful.

NOTES

DECEMBER

DECEMBER CHECKLIST

EARLY

☐ Prune hollies.
☐ Preserve greens from cedar, boxwood or hollies for Christmas.
☐ Prepare sunny location for Christmas plants.
☐ Prepare amaryllis for blooming.
☐ Continue watering evergreens, weather permitting.
☐ Make sure trees are properly staked to prevent wind damage.
☐ Mulch over mums and foxglove.
☐ Clean up garden and rake lawn.

MIDDLE

☐ Provide humidity for houseplants and clean the leaves of houseplants.
☐ Check to make sure roses and strawberries are properly mulched.
☐ Check stored bulbs and corms for disease.
☐ Keep live Christmas tree well-watered and stored in a cool place.

LATE

☐ Use sand, nitrogen fertilizer or ashes on icy sidewalks and driveways.
☐ Don't use salt.
☐ Toss ashes from fireplace onto the garden.
☐ Continue feeding the birds.
☐ Check houseplants for spider mites.

SUPER TIP

☐ Picking a Christmas tree

December is the month when the seed catalogs arrive, gardeners compile a wish list of presents, and poinsettias and cactuses reign as the holiday flowers. It is, after all, only about 60 days until early planting.

December comes from **decem**, the Latin word for ten. December used to have 29 days, but Julius Caesar added two more.

It's usually warmer in December than during other winter months. The average high temperature in this area in December is 45.4 degrees; the average low 28.9 degrees. The average precipitation — including melted snow — is 3.48 degrees.

The most precipitation ever in Louisville in December was 8.43 inches; the least, .65 inches. The highest-ever temperature was 76 degrees on Dec. 3, 1982. The coldest was minus 9 degrees on Dec. 22, 1960.

The normal snowfall in December is 2.6 inches, but 24.6 inches fell in 1917, including 15 inches in 24 hours, the second heaviest snowstorm in Louisville history.

The most snow in Louisville history was the 50.2 inches that fell in 1917-18, with the winter of 1977-78 right behind it. The most snow ever to fall in Louisville on Christmas Eve was the 8.3 inches that fell in 1939.

There are nine hours and 43 minutes of sun on Dec. 1 and nine hours and 34 minutes on Dec. 31. On Dec. 20, the shortest day of the year, there are nine hours and 31 minutes of sun, and most of it is low in the sky.

The average soil temperature in December is between 41 and 46 degrees.

Walt Disney, who gives many people joy around Christmas, was born Dec. 5, 1901, and Eli Whitney, inventor of the cotton gin, was born on Dec. 8, 1765.

EARLY

Now is a good time to prune hollies and use their trimmings for indoor decorating. Prune with care, always keeping in mind the natural pyramid shape of a holly tree. If you do a good job of cutting the branches, your tree will already be pruned for the coming season.

Hollies usually need little pruning except to train a leader or to remove dead, diseased and damaged branches. If several stems develop where you want one leader, remove the other stems. If part of a leader is dead or injured, cut it back to healthy wood just above a bud or leaf. If the entire leader is dead, cut it back to the nearest whorl of branches.

You can control the direction a branch grows by pruning it back to the proper bud, which will point in the direction you want the shoot to grow. If you cut a branch back completely to the trunk, or cut a twig back to the branch, new growth may not appear, so cut back only to a bud.

And if you're curious, yes, there are deciduous holly trees available from some nurseries and garden shops. They are especially beautiful in the fall when their brilliant red berries put on an amazing show of color. There is a fine collection of these trees in Bernheim Forest at Clermont, Ky.

If you cut greens such as cedar, boxwood or hollies for Christmas, soak them thoroughly in a tub of water for 24 hours. Then dip the ends in candle wax to seal them. Magnolia leaves can be clipped and dipped in a container of floor wax. It makes them shiny and seals the leaves so they stay shiny longer.

Chances are you'll be getting — and possibly giving — several of the traditional Christmas plants in the next week or so. Here are a few things you should be doing to care for those plants.

They'll need as much natural light as possible, or their leaves will drop like maple leaves in autumn. Prepare a place with lots of bright light but not in the direct sunlight, which will cause leaves to fade.

Maintain a uniform temperature of 65 to 70 degrees, keep the air as humid as possible, maybe with trays filled with pebbles you can water, but keep the plant's soil on the dry side.

The amaryllis, also a common Christmas gift, requires special care. Many arrive in full bloom, but preplanted amaryllis are also easy to grow from bulbs. Water regularly and grow at average room temperatures near a window or under plant lights. The stalks will lengthen daily, and in four to six weeks you'll have huge, lovely blooms.

Or, if you want to save money, pot a bulb yourself and give the amaryllis as a gift. The bulb likes a tight home, so use a pot about an inch larger than the bulb. The pot should have holes in the bottom, which you want to cover with a layer of coarse material, like pebbles, for good drainage. Plant the bulb in commercial potting soil or a mix of loam and peat moss or vermiculite. Plant so the top half of the bulb is above the surface. Firm the soil and water well.

But after that — and this is very important — water sparingly until the flower stem appears. Let the top inch of soil dry well between waterings. As the stem gets longer, increase the water. When it is ready to bloom, apply water-soluble fertilizer.

Oddly enough, the amaryllis often doesn't send up foliage until the flowers begin to open on the stem. If you're lucky and keep the plant in a sunny room with mild temperatures, it will bloom for a month.

After the blooms fade, keep the plant in a sunny window as the foliage fades. In the spring, set the plant outside in a partly sunny area but keep watering and feeding it. By fall the foliage will yellow. Cut off the leaves, let the plant rest for about a month, then begin the cycle again by washing off some of the old dirt with a garden hose. Give it some new soil, a teaspoon of bone meal and begin the process again. Leave the bulb in the pot for three or four years before repotting.

Weather permitting, keep trying to water your evergreen trees because they will lose moisture through their leaves all winter. Deciduous trees don't need that much water — unless they were newly planted — because they don't have leaves. Don't forget to mulch evergreens too.

Check all sizable deciduous plants that went in the ground this fall or last spring, including fruit and ornamental types, to make certain they are properly staked to resist wind damage. Be sure thin-barked trees such as maples are wrapped with burlap, heavy sisal paper or plastic tree wrap. Be sure to remove that wrap about April.

Continue to place mulches over valued perennials like mums and foxglove to prevent fluctuating winter temperatures from heaving them from the ground. In a few more weeks the limbs of your discarded Christmas tree will shield the plants but not suffocate them.

I hope you have cleaned up the flower and vegetable garden, pulled up all dead tomato and annual flowers and snipped off the blackened top of perennials like peonies all the way down to the ground. Above all, I hope you have raked your lawn so the leaves don't suffocate the grass.

MIDDLE

Check houseplants for brown, dry edges indicating too little humidity in the house. If pebble trays don't work, a humidifier may be a good investment, especially if you plan on increasing your indoor collection. On gloomy days — or weeks — try to move your plants closer to a window. Artificial lighting can help. Reduce watering and withhold fertilizer.

It's also especially important to clean the foliage of your houseplants during the shorter winter days because dust reduces the already diminished light. The easiest way to do this is to set them in the bathtub and squirt them with a fine spray of lukewarm water. Wash your rubby ducky if the mood strikes.

By now you should have protected those precious roses by mounding mulch or dirt over the roses, which should have been cut back to 12 to 14 inches. Strawberries also need a straw mulch by now.

Begin checking your stored canna, gladiolus, dahlia and caladium bulbs and corms to see if any are diseased. Throw out any that look sick. Use a fungicide to protect the rest, although it may be too late.

We've talked several times about preparing a hole in the ground for your living Christmas tree, but now that the time is here you should remember not to keep the tree indoors for more than 10 days because drafts and dryness could kill it. There's also a danger the tree will break dormancy indoors, and putting it outside after that will kill it.

Keep it well-watered indoors. Before planting outdoors let it spend a few days in a cool garage to get readjusted to the cold, cruel world. When planting, water well, stake and mulch.

LATE

As tempting as it is, avoid using salt on sidewalks and driveways, especially near trees and shrubs. Salt injures trees and shrubs. Try sand, nitrogen fertilizer, ashes or better yet, potassium chloride. It will melt ice at temperatures down to 40 degrees below zero, and will not damage plants.

In any case, all remaining ice-melting materials should be removed as soon as the ice is gone.

Speaking of ashes, now is the perfect time to toss all the ashes from your holiday fires onto your garden. In general, good quality, unleached ashes will contain about 5 to 10 percent potash, 1 to 2 percent phosphate and 50 to 70 percent limestone equivalent.

So while there is some benefit in adding wood ashes, you should remember they contain no nitrogen, the most important fertilizing element. But when wood ash is applied at the rate of 40 to 50 pounds per 1,000 square feet — which is easily obtained from a winter of burning wood — it will supply enough potash for most lawns and gardens.

Also, because of its high lime content, ashes should never be dumped around acid-loving plants like azaleas and rhododendrons.

If you've already started feeding birds for the winter, keep it up. While you're at it, an electrically heated bird bath can be a real focal point for birds, your feeder and you.

Keep a sharp eye out for spider-mite invasions of your plants. They love warm, dry air, and regular spraying may be needed to keep your plants safe.

FRED'S TIPS

If you are making a list, checking it twice, trying to find out who's naughty or nice, and you've got a nice gardener on your list, I've got some suggestions for you.

A good gardener can always use tools, like a hand pruner or digging tools. It may cost a little more, but look for sturdiness, durability and balance. I received a set of hand tools a few Christmases back made of solid pieces of aluminum. They are easy to clean and have a "pistol grip" so they do not slip from my grasp.

Consider a "soaker hose," which is the most efficient way to water. The hose has holes punched in it every few inches, allowing the water to drip out directly into the soil instead of gushing out the end.

Hose-attached sprayers are also

useful. One of the best I have ever used is called a "hose sprayer with a metering dial." It has a dial that allows you to attach a bottle to the bottom and monitor exactly how much chemical you use.

Also give houseplants, bulbs that can be forced indoors and even packs of seeds as stocking stuffers. If you want to give live plants, traditional ones such as poinsettia, Christmas cactus, cyclamen, ornamental pepper, Jerusalem cherry and begonia are good. It's an excellent way to say, "Happy holidays, and here's wishing you the happiest of gardening years."

And hey, don't forget this: What could be a better present than a copy of "Fred Wiche's Gardening Almanac"?

Chestnuts are very good eating at Christmas, if you can get to the meat of the matter. To do it, poke a hole in the flat side of the shell, place a bunch in a kitchen pot and cover with boiling water for 15 to 20 minutes. Take out a few at a time to eat; it's easier to get to the meat when they're hot.

For roasting, put them in a heavy skillet in three tablespoons of cooking oil per pound of nuts. Bring them to a sizzle, then stick them in the oven for 20 minutes at 400 degrees. Ummmmmmmm, good.

The rabbit's-foot fern is a good choice for a winter gift because it tolerates dry air better than many other ferns. Give it bright, indirect light and keep it away from drafts. Keep the soil moist but not soggy. Mist once a week

and feed it 20-20-20 fertilizer at half the recommended rate. I can hear it saying, "Ummmmmmm, good!"

Don't leave your insecticides and fungicides outside in the garage or storage shed in cold weather. The ideal storage temperature is 60 degrees or higher. Don't ever let the temperature drop below 40 degrees, which could destroy the chemical combinations and render the spray ineffective.

The following, ranked in order from the most heat-efficient to the least heat-efficient, is a list of commonly available firewood in this area. They are shagbark hickory, black locust, hard maple, apple, white oak, white ash, black walnut, black ash, soft maple and poplar. Be sure you know what you're buying. Gas-station attendants often don't.

If we happen to have a very heavy snowfall, you might go out and trample down the snow around the trunks of your very young fruit trees. It will discourage rodents from moving in to eat; packed snow is hard to bore through.

Bird feeders are great, but you can help birds get through the winter and improve your landscape at the same time by planting shrubs and trees that grow food birds like to eat, as well as providing protection near the feeder. So make a note, and next spring plant some winterberry, scarlet firethorn, chokeberry, sumac, burning bush, crab apple, cotoneaster and viburnum to grow bird food.

Sometimes people have a difficult time keeping their cyclamen healthy and in bloom. Just be sure the soil never becomes dry enough to cause even slight wilting of the plant and flowers. It also does best in half-sunny windows, where there are do drafts, and temperatures from 50 to 70 degrees.

If you're buying an indoor plant in this weather, ask the salesperson to wrap it in floral wrapping to protect it from the cold and chill. Preheat your car to prevent chill injury. Never leave it in an unattended car while shopping. Make the nursery your last stop before heading home.

I keep an old bucket of oily sand in my tool shed to use in cleaning my tools. Every time I change oil in a piece of lawn or gardening equipment I pour the oil in the sand. The abrasive action does a wonderful job of cleaning off the dirt, and the oil provides protection against rust.

If your fuchsia plant made it through the summer, it needs to be "winterized." Cut the stems back to eight inches in length, keep the growing medium quite dry through the winter, give it some light and keep the temperature cool but not freezing. Next spring resume watering and feeding.

To prevent stored fertilizer from absorbing moisture and turning into "Christmas cake," place it in a sealed plastic bag or waterproof container with a snug-fitting lid. Store in a dry location.

FRED'S SUPER TIP

Every year about now an uncommon sight presents itself on the wind-swept, forested hillsides of Kentuckiana. Hundreds of city folk, spurred by the romance of cutting down a yule tree, descend upon tree farms to play Paul Bunyan.

The idea is that you drive into the country to saw down a Christmas tree. It should be fun rather than frustrating. So here is some advice:

1. It is always a good idea to telephone the tree farm ahead of time to make sure of the supply — especially if you wait until Christmas Eve.

2. A thermos filled with hot chocolate or coffee can help ease the sting of a biting wind.

3. Bring cash. Farms don't

have machines that accept credit cards. And checks may be frowned upon.

4. Wear warm clothes. This isn't as obvious as it sounds. City folk are often surprised by the chill out on the back 40. Don't wear your Sunday-go-to-meetin' shoes, especially if there's been a lot of rain. It's going to be muddy, so wear shoes with good traction.

5. Bring a saw if you can. Loaners generally are available but expect a waiting line for one. Hatchets and axes are not recommended. They are inferior to saws in cutting trees and are like a time bomb for the accident-prone.

6. Then there is twine. You will need some to bind the tree to the car. (Don't forget: stump end toward the front bumper. Reverse it and even at 55 mph you will be decorating the highway with pine branches all the way home.) And if you're driving one of those little compact cars, don't expect to bring home a giant of the woods. You are liable to scare someone to death when they see this big tree coming at them in the rear-view mirror.

7. And finally, remember that trees always look smaller when you see them in the great outdoors. So before starting out, measure the space in the room that the tree will occupy. There's no point in going out and cutting a 14-foot tree if you are going to have to lop four feet off the bottom when you get it home.

If you intend to buy your tree from a corner lot, here are some guidelines to follow in making your selection.

1. Be sure the tree has needles that are relatively pliant and firmly attached to the twigs. If the needles are brittle and tend to snap or shatter when bent between your fingers, the tree may be dry or frozen, depending on weather conditions.

2. When you get the tree home, cut off 1 or 1 1/2 inches from the butt and promptly stand the tree in a pail of fresh warm water. The amount of water consumed can vary considerably, depending on the species, condition and size of the tree and on the temperatures and relative humidity of the room.

If the tree is six to seven feet tall and if room temperature and humidity are average for early December, you might discover that a good tree can take up a pint of water during a 24-hour period.

3. Keep water in the Christmas-tree stand at all times. A big tree may use two quarts of water during the first 24 hours it is inside and may average a quart of more a day for the first week. A freshly cut tree may take up considerably less water.

4. For several years I have doused our Christmas tree with an anti-dessicant spray called "Wilt-Proof" before bringing it inside. This material seals the needles, prevents moisture from being lost, and keeps the tree fresher longer. It seems to have helped a lot, but always remember; there is no such thing as a fireproof Christmas tree.

So have a safe holiday, and Merry Christmas from our house to yours!

NOTES

INDEX

Z

TIMES FOR SIDEDRESSING VEGETABLES

Crop	Time of Application
Asparagus	Before growth starts in spring.
Beans	After heavy blossom and set of pods.
Beets	Additional nitrogen might reduce yield or lower quality.
Broccoli	3 weeks after transplanting.
Cabbage	3 weeks after transplanting.
Cauliflower	3 weeks after transplanting.
Carrots	Additional nitrogen might reduce yield or lower quality.
Cucumbers	Apply 1 week after blossoming begins and same amount 3 weeks later.
Eggplant	After first fruit set.
Kale	When plants are about one-third grown.
Lettuce	Additional nitrogen might reduce yield or lower quality.
Muskmelons	Apply 1 week after blossoming begins and same amount 3 weeks later.
Onions	1 to 2 weeks after bulb formation starts.
Parsnips	Additional nitrogen might reduce yield or lower quality.
Peas	After heavy bloom and set of pods.
Peppers	After first fruit set.
Potatoes	After tuber formation starts (bloom stage), about 6 weeks after planting.
Spinach	When plants are about one-third grown.
Squash	Additional nitrogen might reduce yield or lower quality.
Sweet corn	When plants are 12 inches tall.
Sweet potatoes	Additional nitrogen might reduce yield or lower quality.
Tomatoes	Apply 1 to 2 weeks before first picking and same amount 2 weeks after first picking.
Turnips	Additional nitrogen might reduce yield or lower quality.
Watermelon	Additional nitrogen might reduce yield or lower quality.

Source: University of Kentucky, College of Agriculture

VEGETABLE PLANTING GUIDE

Crop	Number of Transplants or Seeds Per Foot	Distance Between Plants When Thinned or Transplanted (inches)	Distance Between Rows (inches)	Planting Depth (inches)
Asparagus	1 crown	18	30	6-8
Beans, bush, lima	6-8 seeds	3-4	30	1-2
Beans, bush, snap	8 seeds	2-3	30	1-2
Beets	10 seeds	4	12-18	½-1
Broccoli	1 transplant	18	30	
Brussels sprouts	1 transplant per 2 ft.	18-24	36	
Cabbage	1 transplant	12-18	30	
Carrots	15-20 seeds	2-3	12-18	½
Cauliflower	1 transplant	18	30	
Cucumbers	3-4 seeds	6-12	30-48	½-1
Kale	4-6 seeds	8-12	18-30	½
Kohlrabi	6-8 seeds	3-6	18-30	½
Lettuce, head	1 transplant	12-15	18-24	½
Lettuce, leaf	10-20 seeds	1-2	12-18	½
Muskmelons	2-3 seeds or 1 transplant	24	30-48	½-1
Okra	3 seeds	12-15	30	1
Onions, from seed	10-15 seeds	2-4	12-18	½-1
Onions	3-6 transplants or sets	2-4	12-18	2-3
Parsley	10-15 seeds	4-6	12-18	½
Parsnips	15-20 seeds	3-4	18-30	½-1
Peas	10-12 seeds	Do not thin	30	2
Peppers	1 transplant	18	30	
Potatoes	1 seed piece	10-12	30	4
Pumpkins	1-2 seeds	10-12 ft.	72	1
Radishes, spring	10-15 seeds	1	12-18	½
Rhubarb	1 crown per 2 ft.	24	30	
Spinach	12-15 seeds	2-4	12-30	½
Squash, summer	2-3 seeds in hill	24	30	
Sweet corn	2-3 seeds	9-12, single plants	30	1-2
Sweet potatoes	1 slip	12-18	30	
Tomatoes	1 transplant per 2 ft.	18-24	30	
Watermelons	1-2 seeds in row	6-8 ft.	72	1

CRITICAL TIMES TO WATER VEGETABLES

Vegetable	Critical period of water needs
Asparagus	Fern growth
Bean, lima	Pollination and pod development
Bean, snap	Pod enlargement
Broccoli	Establishment, head development
Cabbage	Establishment, head development
Carrot	Establishment, root enlargement
Cauliflower	Establishment, head development
Corn, sweet	Silking, tasseling and ear development
Cucumber	Flowering and fruit development
Eggplant	Uniform supply from flowering through harvest
Melon	Fruit set and early development
Onion, dry	Bulb enlargement
Pea	Flowering and seed enlargement
Pepper	Uniform supply from flowering through harvest
Potato	Tuber set and tuber enlargement
Radish	Root enlargement
Squash, summer	Bud development, flowering and fruit development
Tomato	Uniform supply from flowering through harvest
Turnip	Root enlargement

Source: University of Kentucky, College of Agriculture

BULB PLANTING GUIDE

Flowering Time	Planting Depth (inches)	Spacing (inches)	Flowering Height (inches)
Early Spring			
Snowdrops	5	3	Up to 6
Winter Aconite	5	3	Up to 6
Iris Reticulata	5	3	Up to 6
Crocus	5	3	Up to 6
Anemone Blanda	5	3	Up to 6
Kaufmanniana Tulip	8	6	Up to 6
Fosteriana Tulip	8	6	6 to 12
Single Early Tulip	8	6	6 to 12
Double Early Tulip	8	6	6 to 12
Miniature Daffodil	8	4	6 to 12
Hyacinths	8	6	6 to 12
Trumpet Daffodil	8	6	12 to 20
Mid-Spring			
Triumph Tulip	8	5	12 to 20
Daffodils	8	6	12 to 20
Darwin Hybrid Tulip	8	6	20 to 28
Greigii Tulip	8	6	6 to 20
Fritillaria Imperialis	8	12	Over 28
Late Spring			
Parrot Tulip	8	6	12 to 20
Double Late Tulip	8	6	12 to 20
Lily-Flowered Tulip	8	6	20 to 28
Darwin Tulip	8	6	20 to 28
Cottage Tulip	8	6	20 to 28
Rembrandt Tulip	8	6	20 to 28
Spanish Bluebells	5	6	6 to 12
Dutch Iris	8	4	12 to 20
Allium Giganteum	8	8	Over 28

COMMON GARDEN INSECTS

Cutworms

Colorado Potato Beetle

Root Maggots

Mexican Bean Beetle

Imported Cabbageworm

Cucumber Beetle

Mites

Corn Earworm

Cabbage Looper

Squash Vine Borers

Stalk Borer

Hornworm

Leafhoppers

Flea Beetle

Japanese Beetle

Aphids

Wireworms

Source: University of Kentucky, College of Agriculture

CROP TIMETABLE

░░░ Growing Time   ██████ Harvest Time

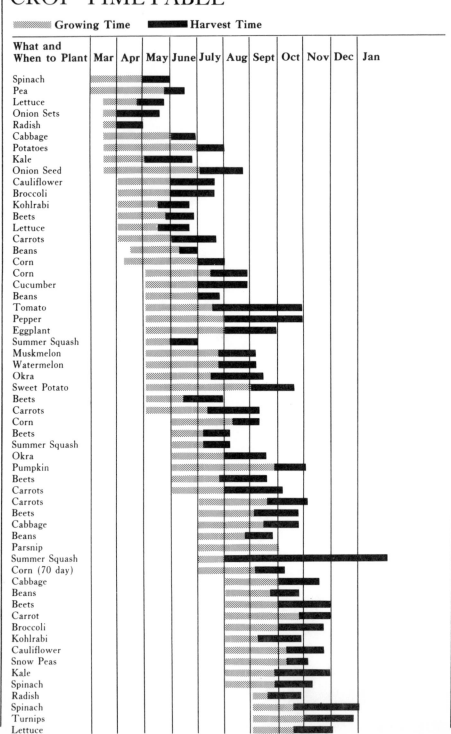

What and When to Plant	Mar	Apr	May	June	July	Aug	Sept	Oct	Nov	Dec	Jan
Spinach											
Pea											
Lettuce											
Onion Sets											
Radish											
Cabbage											
Potatoes											
Kale											
Onion Seed											
Cauliflower											
Broccoli											
Kohlrabi											
Beets											
Lettuce											
Carrots											
Beans											
Corn											
Corn											
Cucumber											
Beans											
Tomato											
Pepper											
Eggplant											
Summer Squash											
Muskmelon											
Watermelon											
Okra											
Sweet Potato											
Beets											
Carrots											
Corn											
Beets											
Summer Squash											
Okra											
Pumpkin											
Beets											
Carrots											
Carrots											
Beets											
Cabbage											
Beans											
Parsnip											
Summer Squash											
Corn (70 day)											
Cabbage											
Beans											
Beets											
Carrot											
Broccoli											
Kohlrabi											
Cauliflower											
Snow Peas											
Kale											
Spinach											
Radish											
Spinach											
Turnips											
Lettuce											

Sure, we'll be more than happy to mail you another copy of Fred Wiche's Gardening Almanac just in case you've worn out this one or would like to buy a copy for a friend. The almanac is the perfect gift for any gardener. Fill out the form below, and we'll mail them anywhere in the United States.

Remember to include a check or money order for each book. The cost is $12.95, plus $2 postage and handling, for each book. Make the check or money order out to Green Thumb Publishing, PO Box 3703, Louisville, Ky., 40201.

If you have any questions call 502-454-7294

ORDER FORM

Please send me_____ copies of "Fred Wiche's Gardening Almanac."

Fred Wiche's Gardening Almanac
$12.95 + $2.00 (Postage & handling) x _____

Amount enclosed $ _____

Name

Address

City   State   Zip

Please send_____gift copies of "Fred Wiche's Gardening Almanac" to the following person:

Name

Address

City   State   Zip

Fred Wiche's Gardening Almanac
$12.95 + $2.00 (Postage & handling) x _____

Amount enclosed $_____

Fill out this card and we'll be happy to include it with your gift.

TO:_____

FROM:_____